Develop Super Power Memory

Published by :
Lotus Press Publishers & Distributors

Develop Super Power Memory

Neha Mathur

Lotus PRESS

4735/22, Prakash Deep Building
Ansari Road, Darya Ganj,
New Delhi - 110002

Lotus Press : Publishers & Distributors
Unit No. 220, 2nd Floor, 4735/22, Prakash Deep Building,
Ansari Road, Darya Ganj, New Delhi- 110002
Ph.: 41325510, 98118-38000
• E-mail : lotuspress1984@gmail.com
www.lotuspress.co.in

Develop Super Power Memory

ISBN: 978-81-8382-223-7

Printed & Published by : **Lotus Press Publisher & Distributors,** New Delhi-02

PREFACE

Memory is one of the most basic and important functions of the human brain. In fact, without memory we can't learn.

Most people think of memory as how we recall past events, but it is also the building blocks for almost everything we do in the present and future.

Our memories provide us with a sense of our own personality and give us the information we need to function properly in the everyday world.

Communication, problem solving and relationships all rely to some extent on memories that we use to inform us as we take action.

Of course, our brains can't remember everything. Brains simply don't have the capacity; if they tried to remember everything we experienced, there wouldn't be room for anything else.

Involuntary muscle function, thought processes, the senses and numerous other activities would be crowded out. There are dozens of variables that affect how much we remember, how long we retain it and whether we can recall it.

Fortunately, we can learn ways to improve how much we remember and enhance how long we remember it. Therefore, present work, namely, ***Develop Super Power Memory*** has been prepared.

Positive and enlightened feedback is solicited.

Author

CONTENTS

CHAPTER 1

What is Memory

In psychology, memory is an organism's mental ability to store, retain and recall information. Traditional studies of memory began in the fields of philosophy, including techniques of artificially enhancing the memory. The late nineteenth and early twentieth century put memory within the paradigms of cognitive psychology. In recent decades, it has become one of the principal pillars of a branch of science called cognitive neuroscience, an interdisciplinary link between cognitive psychology and neuroscience.

Processes

From information processing perspective there are three main stages in the formation and retrieval of memory:

- *Encoding* or registration (receiving, processing and combining of received information)
- *Storage* (creation of a permanent record of the encoded information)

- *Retrieval* or *recall* (calling back the stored information in response to some cue for use in a process or activity)

Sensory Memory

Sensory memory is the ability to retain impressions of sensory information after the original stimulus has ceased. It refers to items detected by the sensory receptors which are retained temporarily in the sensory registers and which have a large capacity for unprocessed information but are only able to hold accurate images of sensory information momentarily.

The two types of sensory memory that have been most explored are iconic memory and echoic memory.

Classification

Sensory memory is still considered to operate within this approximate time frame (less than 1 second and no more than 2 seconds) and so is very short lived. It is also characterised by being outside of conscious control (i.e. it happens automatically and unbidden).

Despite retaining information for a very short period of time, it is not to be confused with short-term memory (which typically lasts 10-15 seconds without rehearsal of the remembered material) and is so named to distinguish it from long-term memory which can store information for as long as a lifetime.

Short-term Memory

Short-term memory (sometimes referred to as "primary memory" or "active memory") refers to the capacity for holding a small amount of information in mind in an active, readily available state for a short period of time. The duration of short-term memory (when rehearsal is prevented) is assumed to be in the order of seconds. Estimates of the capacity of short-term memory vary – from about 3 or 4 elements (i.e., words, digits, or letters) to about 9 elements. A commonly-cited capacity is 7±2 elements. In contrast, long-term memory indefinitely stores a seemingly unlimited amount of information.

Existence of a Separate Store

A classical model of memory developed in the 1960s assumed that all memories pass from a short-term to a long-term store after a small period of time.

This model is referred to as the "modal model" and has been most famously detailed by Shiffrin. The exact mechanisms by which this transfer takes place, whether all or only some memories are retained permanently, and indeed the existence of a genuine distinction between the two stores, remain controversial topics among experts.

One form of evidence, cited in favour of the separate existence of a short-term store comes from anterograde amnesia, the inability to learn new facts and episodes. Patients with this form of amnesia, have intact ability to retain small amounts of information over short time scales (up to 30 seconds) but are dramatically impaired in their ability to form longer-term memories.

This is interpreted as showing that the short-term store is spared from amnesia. A memory can remain in your short-term memory bank for a total of 20 seconds.

Other evidence comes from experimental studies showing that some manipulations (e.g., a distracter task, such as repeatedly subtracting a single-digit number from a larger number following learning) impair memory for the 3 to 5 most recently learned words of a list (presumably still held in short-term memory), while leaving recall for words from earlier in the list (presumably stored in long-term memory) unaffected; other manipulations (e.g., semantic similarity of the words) affect only memory for earlier list words, but do not affect memory for the last few words in a list.

These results show that different factors affect short-term recall (disruption of rehearsal) and long-term recall (semantic similarity). Together, these findings show that long-term memory and short-term memory can vary independently of each other.

Not all researchers agree that short-term and long-term memories are separate systems. Some theorists propose that memory is unitary over all time scales, from milliseconds to years.

Support for the unitary memory hypothesis comes from the fact that it has been difficult to demarcate a clear boundary between short-term and long-term memory.

For instance, Tarnow shows that the recall probability *vs.* latency curve is a straight line from 6 to 600 seconds, with the probability of failure to recall only saturating after 600 seconds. If there were really two different memory stores operating in this time frame, one could expect a discontinuity in this curve.

Other research has shown that the detailed pattern of recall errors looks remarkably similar for recall of a list immediately after learning (presumably from short-term memory) and recall after 24 hours (necessarily from long-term memory).

Duration of Short-term Memory

The limited duration of short-term memory immediately suggests that its contents spontaneously decay over time. The decay assumption is part of many theories of short-term memory, most notably Baddeley's model of working memory. The decay assumption is usually paired with the idea of rapid covert rehearsal: In order to overcome the limitation of short-term memory, and retain information for longer, information must be periodically repeated, or rehearsed — either by articulating it out loud, or by mentally simulating such articulation. In this way, the information will re-enter the short-term store and be retained for a further period.

Several researchers, however, dispute that spontaneous decay plays any significant role in forgetting over the short-term , and the evidence is far from conclusive.

Authors doubting that decay causes forgetting from short-term memory often offer as an alternative some form of interference: When several elements (such as digits, words, or pictures) are held in short-term memory simultaneously, their representations compete with each other for recall, or degrade each other.

Thereby, new content gradually pushes out older content, unless the older content is actively protected against interference by rehearsal or by directing attention to it.

Capacity of Short-term Memory

Whatever the cause or causes of forgetting over the short-term may be, there is consensus that it severely limits the amount of new information that we can retain over brief periods of time. This limit is referred to as the finite capacity of short-term memory.

The capacity of short-term memory is often called memory span, in reference to a common procedure of measuring it. In a memory span test, the experimenter presents lists of items (e.g. digits or words) of increasing length. An individual's span is determined as the longest list length that he or she can recall correctly in the given order on at least half of all trials.

In an early and highly influential article, George Miller suggested that human short-term memory has a forward memory span of approximately seven items plus or minus two. More recent research has shown that this "magical number seven" is roughly accurate for college students recalling lists of digits, but memory span varies widely with populations tested and with material used.

For example, the ability to recall words in order depends on a number of characteristics of these words: fewer words can be recalled when the words have longer spoken duration; this is known as the *word-length effect*, or when their speech sounds are similar to each other; this is called the *phonological similarity effect*. More words can be recalled when the words are highly familiar or occur frequently in the language.

Recall performance is also better when all of the words in a list are taken from a single semantic category (such as sports) than when the words are taken from different categories. According to the available evidence, the best overall estimate of short-term memory is about four pieces or "chunks" of information.

Chunking: Chunking is the process with which we can expand our ability to remember things in the short term. Chunking is also a process by which a person organises material into meaningful groups.

Although the average person may only retain about four different units in short-term memory, chunking can greatly increase a person's recall capacity.

For example, in recalling a phone number, the person could chunk the digits into three groups: first, the area code (such as 215), then a three-digit chunk (123) and lastly a four-digit chunk (4567).

This method of remembering phone numbers is far more effective than attempting to remember a string of 10 digits.

Practice and the usage of existing information in long-term memory can lead to additional improvements in one's ability to use chunking.

Long-term Memory

Long-term memory (LTM) is memory that can last as little as a few days or as long as decades. It differs structurally and functionally from working memory or short-term memory, which ostensibly stores items for only around 18 seconds. Biologically, short-term memory is a temporary potentiation of neural connections that can become long-term memory through the process of rehearsal and meaningful association.

Much is not known about the underlying biological mechanisms of long-term memory, but the process of long-term potentiation, which involves a physical change in the structure of neurons, has been proposed as the mechanism by which short-term memories move into long-term storage. Notably, the time scale involved at each level of memory processing remains under investigation.

As long-term memory is subject to fading in the natural

forgetting process, several recalls/retrievals of memory may be needed for long-term memories to last for years, dependent also on the depth of processing. Individual retrievals can take place in increasing intervals in accordance with the principle of spaced repetition. This can happen quite naturally through reflection or deliberate recall often dependent on the perceived importance of the material.

Encoding of Information

Long-term memory encodes information semantically for storage, as researched by Baddeley. However, there is some evidence that proves that long-term memory also encodes by sound for storage.

An example of this is when one experiences the "tip of the tongue" state in which one cannot remember a particular word, but they know it sounds similar to another word. The target word is said to be on the tip of the tongue. It is almost grasped, but not totally. This has nothing to do with meaning but with what the word sounds like.

Sleep

Some theories consider sleep to be an important factor in establishing well-organised long-term memories.

According to Tarnow's theory, long-term memories are stored in dream format. During waking life an executive function interprets long-term memory consistent with reality checking.

Types of Memory

The brain does not store memories in one unified structure, as might be seen in a computer's hard disk drive. Instead, different types of memory are stored in different regions of the brain. LTM is typically divided up into two major headings: declarative memory and implicit memory (or procedural memory).

1. Declarative memory refers to all memories that are consciously available. These are encoded by the hippocampus, entorhinal cortex, and perirhinal cortex, but consolidated and stored elsewhere. The precise location of storage is unknown, but the temporal cortex has been proposed as a likely candidate. Declarative memory also has two major subdivisions:

   - Episodic memory refers to memory for specific events in time
   - Semantic memory refers to knowledge about the external world, such as the function of a pencil.

2. Procedural memory refers to the use of objects or movements of the body, such as how exactly to use a pencil or ride a bicycle. This type of memory is encoded and probably stored by the cerebellum and the striatum.

There are various other categorisations of memory and types of memory that have captured research interest. Prospective memory (its complement: retrospective memory) is an example.

Emotional memory, the memory for events that evoke a particularly strong emotion, is another. Emotion and memory is a domain that can involve both declarative and procedural memory processes. Emotional memories are consciously available, but elicit a powerful, unconscious physiological reaction.

They also have a unique physiological pathway that involves strong connections from the amygdala into the prefrontal cortex, but much weaker connections running back from the prefrontal cortex to the amgydala.

Disorders of Memory

Minor everyday slips and lapses of memory are fairly commonplace, and may increase naturally with age, when ill, or when under stress.

Some women may experience more memory lapses following the onset of the menopause. More serious problems with memory generally occur due to traumatic brain injury or neurodegenerative disease:

Everyday memory problems: The everyday experience of memory problems is the problem of failed recall, forgetting. The tip-of-the-tongue phenomenon is particularly frustrating because the person trying to remember feels that the memory is available.

In physical terms your neurons are firing, but your receptors aren't catching. Failing to remember something in the situation in which it would have been useful leads to regret.

Traumatic brain injury: The majority of findings about memory have been the result of studies that lesioned specific brain regions in rats or primates, but some of the most important work has been the result of accidental or inadvertent brain trauma.

Neurodegenerative diseases: Many neurodegenerative diseases can cause memory loss. Some of the most prevalent (and consequently, most intensely researched) include Alzheimer's Disease, Dementia, Huntington's Disease, Multiple Sclerosis, and Parkinson's Disease. None act specifically on memory; instead memory loss is often a casualty of generalised neuronal deterioration. Currently, these illnesses are irreversible, but research into stem cells, psychopharmacology, and genetic engineering hold much promise.

Models

Models of memory provide abstract representations of how memory is believed to work. Below are several models proposed over the years by various psychologists from all over the World. Note that there is some controversy as to whether there are several memory structures, for example, Tarnow (2005) finds that it is likely that there is only one memory structure between 6 and 600 seconds.

Atkinson-Shiffrin Model

The multi-store model (also known as Atkinson-Shiffrin memory model) was first recognised in 1968 by Atkinson and Shiffrin.

The multi-store model has been criticised for being too simplistic. For instance, long-term memory is believed to be actually made up of multiple subcomponents, such as episodic and procedural memory. It also proposes that rehearsal is the only mechanism by which information eventually reaches long-term storage, but evidence shows us capable of remembering things without rehearsal.

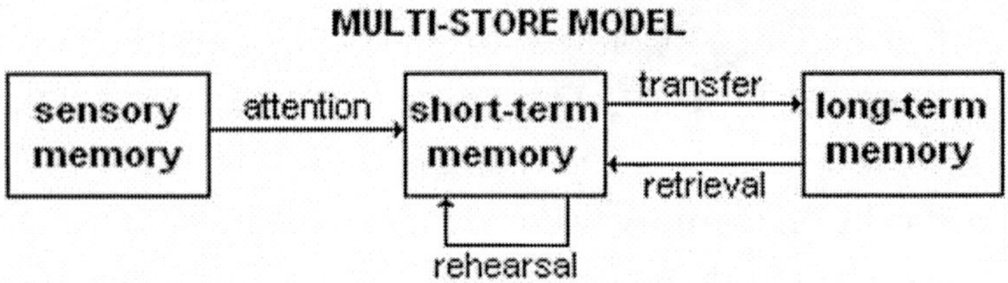

The model also shows all the memory stores as being a single unit whereas research into this shows different. For example, short-term memory can be broken up into different units such as visual information and acoustic information. Patient KF proves this. Patient KF was brain damaged and had problems with his short-term memory. He had problems with things such as spoken numbers, letters and words and with significant sounds (such as doorbells and cats meowing). Other parts of STM were unaffected, such as visual (pictures).

It also shows the sensory store as a single unit whilst we know that the sensory store is split up into several different parts such as taste, vision, and hearing.

Working Memory

Working memory (also referred to as short-term memory, depending on the specific theory) is a theoretical construct within cognitive psychology that refers to the structures and processes used for temporarily storing and manipulating information.

There are numerous theories as to both the theoretical structure of working memory as well as to the specific parts of the brain responsible for working memory.

However, most researchers agree that the frontal cortex, parietal cortex, anterior cingulate, and parts of the basal ganglia are crucial for functioning. Much of the understanding of the neural basis of working memory has come from lesion experiments in animals and imaging experiments in humans.

History

The term was first used in the 1960s in the context of theories that likened the mind to a computer. Atkinson and Shiffrin used this term, "working memory" to describe their "short-term store." What we now call working memory was referred to as a "short-term store" or short-term memory, primary memory, immediate memory, operant memory, or provisional memory.

Short-term memory is the ability to remember information over a brief period of time (in the order of seconds). Most theorists today use the concept of working memory to replace or include the older concept of short-term memory, thereby marking a stronger emphasis on the notion of manipulation of information instead of passive maintenance.

The earliest mention of experiments on the neural basis of working memory can be traced back to over 100 years ago, when Hitzig and Ferrier described ablation experiments of the prefrontal cortex (PFC). They concluded that the frontal cortex was important for cognitive processes rather than sensory ones.

Jacobsen and colleagues were the first to conclude that the cognitive processes in the PFC were notable in delay-dependent tasks; in other words, they suffered from short-term memory loss.

Working Memory Capacity

Working memory is generally considered to have limited capacity. The earliest quantification of the capacity limit associated with short-term memory was the "magical number seven" introduced by Miller. He noticed that the memory span of young adults was around seven elements, called chunks, regardless whether the elements were digits, letters, words, or other units.

Later research revealed that span does depend on the category of chunks used (e.g., span is around seven for digits, around six for letters, and around five for words), and even on features of the chunks within a category. For instance, span is lower for long words than for short words. In general, memory span for verbal contents (digits, letters, words, etc.) strongly depends on the time it takes to speak the contents aloud, and on the lexical status of the contents (i.e., whether the contents are words known to the person or not). Several other factors also affect a person's measured span, and therefore it is difficult to pin down the capacity of short-term or working memory to a number of chunks.

Nonetheless, Cowan has proposed that working memory has a capacity of about four chunks in young adults (and fewer in children and old adults).

Measures of working-memory capacity and their correlates: Working memory capacity can be tested by a variety of tasks. A commonly used measure is a dual-task paradigm combining a memory span measure with a concurrent processing task, sometimes referred to as "complex span". Daneman and Carpenter invented the first version of this kind of task, the "reading span". Subjects read a number of sentences (usually between 2 and 6) and try to remember the last word of each sentence.

At the end of the list of sentences, they repeat back the

words in their correct order. Other tasks that don't have this dual-task nature have also been shown to be good measures of working memory capacity. The question of what features a task must have to qualify as a good measure of working memory capacity is a topic of ongoing research.

Measures of working-memory capacity are strongly related to performance in other complex cognitive tasks such as reading comprehension, problem solving, and with any measures of the intelligence quotient. Some researchers have argued that working memory capacity reflects the efficiency of executive functions, most notably the ability to maintain a few task-relevant representations in the face of distracting irrelevant information. The tasks seem to reflect individual differences in ability to focus and maintain attention, particularly when other events are serving to capture attention. These effects seem to be a function of frontal brain areas.

Others have argued that the capacity of working memory is better characterised as the ability to mentally form relations between elements, or to grasp relations in given information. This idea has been advanced, among others, by Graeme Halford, who illustrated it by our limited ability to understand statistical interactions between variables.

These authors asked people to compare written statements about the relations between several variables to graphs illustrating the same or a different relation, for example "If the cake is from France then it has more sugar if it is made with chocolate than if it is made with cream but if the cake is from Italy then it has more sugar if it is made with cream than if it is made of chocolate".

This statement describes a relation between three variables

(country, ingredient, and amount of sugar), which most of us can understand. The capacity limit apparent here is obviously not a memory limit – all relevant information can be seen continuously – but a limit on how many relationships we can discern simultaneously.

Training of Working Memory

One theory of attention-deficit hyperactivity disorder states that ADHD can lead to deficits in working memory. Recent studies suggest that working memory can be improved by training in ADHD patients through the Cogmed computerised programme developed by Torkel Klingberg and his colleagues at the Karolinska Institute in Sweden. This random controlled study has found that a period of working memory training increases a range of cognitive abilities and increases IQ test scores.

Consequently, this study supports previous findings suggesting that working memory underlies general intelligence. Another study of the same group has shown that, after training, measured brain activity related to working memory increased in the prefrontal cortex, an area that many researchers have associated with working memory functions. A further study has shown that training with a working memory task (the dual n-back task) improves performance on a certain fluid intelligence test in healthy young adults.

Further research is required to verify whether improving or augmenting the brain's working memory ability increases fluid intelligence.

In 2009, it was reported in Science that working memory training led to measurable density changes for cortical dopamine neuroreceptors in test persons.

How does the brain maintain memories over the short-term?: Much has been learned over the last two decades on where in the brain working memory functions are carried out. Much less is known on how the brain accomplishes short-term maintenance and goal-directed manipulation of information. The persistent firing of certain neurons in the delay period of working memory tasks shows that the brain has a mechanism of keeping representations active without external input.

Keeping representations active, however, is not enough if the task demands maintaining more than one chunk of information. In addition, the components and features of each chunk must be bound together to prevent them from being mixed up. For example, if a red triangle and a green square must be remembered at the same time, one must make sure that "red" is bound to "triangle" and "green" is bound to "square".

One way of establishing such bindings is by having the neurons that represent features of the same chunk fire in synchrony, and those that represent features belonging to different chunks fire out of sync. In the example, neurons representing redness would fire in synchrony with neurons representing the triangular shape, but out of sync with those representing the square shape.

So far, there is no direct evidence that working memory uses this binding mechanism, and other mechanisms have been proposed as well. It has been speculated that synchronous firing of neurons involved in working memory oscillate with frequencies in the theta band (4 to 8 Hz). Indeed, the power of theta frequency in the EEG increases with working memory load, and oscillations in the theta band measured over different parts of the skull become more coordinated when the person tries to remember the binding between two components of information.

Working Memory and Learning

There is now extensive evidence that working memory is linked to key learning outcomes in literacy and numeracy. In a recent large-scale screening study, one in ten children in mainstream classrooms were identified with working memory deficits. The majority of them performed very poorly in academic achievements, independent of their IQ.

Without appropriate intervention, these children lag behind their peers. Recent research has also confirmed that working memory capacity, but not IQ, predicts learning outcomes two years later.

This suggests that working memory impairments are associated with low learning outcomes and constitute a high risk factor for educational under achievement for children. In children with learning disabilities such as dyslexia, ADHD, and developmental coordination disorder, a similar pattern is evident.

In a classroom, common characteristics of working memory impairment include a failure to remember instructions and an inability to complete learning activities. Without early diagnosis, working memory impairment negatively impacts a child's performance throughout their scholastic career.

Research

Today there are hundreds of research laboratories around the world studying various aspects of working memory. There are numerous applications of working memory in the field, such as using working memory capacity to explain intelligence, success at emotion regulation, and other cognitive abilities, furthering the understanding of autism, ADHD, motor dyspraxia, and improving teaching methods,, and creating artificial intelligence based on the human brain.

Levels of Processing

Craik and Lockhart proposed that it is the method and depth of processing that affects how an experience is stored in memory, rather than rehearsal.

- **Organisation** - Mandler gave participants a pack of word cards and asked them to sort them into any number of piles using any system of categorisation they liked.

  When they were later asked to recall as many of the words as they could, those who used more categories remembered more words. This study suggested that the act of organising information makes it more memorable.

- **Distinctiveness** - Eysenck and Eysenck asked participants to say words in a distinctive way, e.g. spell the words out loud. Such participants recalled the words better than those who simply read them off a list.

- **Effort** - Tyler *et al.* had participants solve a series of anagrams, some easy (FAHTER) and some difficult (HREFAT). The participants recalled the difficult anagrams better, presumably because they put more effort into them.

- **Elaboration** - Palmere *et al.* gave participants descriptive paragraphs of a fictitious African nation. There were some short paragraphs and some with extra sentences elaborating the main idea. Recall was higher for the ideas in the elaborated paragraphs.

Classification by Information Type

Anderson divides long-term memory into *declarative (explicit)* and *procedural (implicit)* memories.

Declarative memory requires conscious recall, in that some conscious process must call back the information. It is sometimes called *explicit memory*, since it consists of information that is explicitly stored and retrieved.

Declarative memory can be further sub-divided into semantic memory, which concerns facts taken independent of context; and episodic memory, which concerns information specific to a particular context, such as a time and place.

Semantic memory allows the encoding of abstract knowledge about the world, such as "Delhi is the capital of India". Episodic memory, on the other hand, is used for more personal memories, such as the sensations, emotions, and personal associations of a particular place or time. Autobiographical memory – memory for particular events within one's own life – is generally viewed as either equivalent to, or a subset of, episodic memory.

Visual memory is part of memory preserving some characteristics of our senses pertaining to visual experience. One is able to place in memory information that resembles objects, places, animals or people in sort of a mental image.

Visual memory can result in priming and it is assumed

some kind of perceptual representational system underlies this phenomenon.

In contrast, procedural memory (or *implicit memory*) is not based on the conscious recall of information, but on implicit learning. Procedural memory is primarily employed in learning motor skills and should be considered a subset of implicit memory.

It is revealed when one does better in a given task due only to repetition – no new explicit memories have been formed, but one is unconsciously accessing aspects of those previous experiences. Procedural memory involved in motor learning depends on the cerebellum and basal ganglia.

Topographic memory is the ability to orient oneself in space, to recognise and follow an itinerary, or to recognise familiar places. Getting lost when traveling alone is an example of the failure of topographic memory. This is often reported among elderly patients who are evaluated for dementia. The disorder could be caused by multiple impairments, including difficulties with perception, orientation, and memory.

Classification by Temporal Direction

A further major way to distinguish different memory functions is whether the content to be remembered is in the past, retrospective memory, or whether the content is to be remembered in the future, prospective memory.

Thus, retrospective memory as a category includes semantic memory and episodic/autobiographical memory. In contrast, prospective memory is memory for future intentions, or *remembering to remember*. Prospective memory can be further broken down into event- and time-based prospective remembering. Time-based prospective memories are triggered by a time-cue, such as going to the doctor (action) at 4pm (cue). Event-based prospective memories are intentions triggered by cues, such as remembering to post a letter (action) after seeing a mailbox (cue). Cues do not need to be related to the action (as the mailbox example is), and lists, sticky-notes, knotted handkerchiefs, or string around the finger are all examples of cues that are produced by people as a strategy to enhance prospective memory.

Physiology

Overall, the physiological mechanisms behind memory are poorly understood. Brain areas such as the hippocampus, the amygdala, the striatum, or the mammillary bodies are thought to be involved in specific types of memory. For example, the hippocampus is believed to be involved in spatial learning and declarative learning, while the amygdala is thought to be involved in emotional memory. Damage to certain areas in patients and animal models and subsequent memory deficits is a primary source of information.

However, rather than implicating a specific area, it could be that damage to adjacent areas, or to a pathway traveling through the area is actually responsible for the observed deficit. Further, it is not sufficient to describe memory, and its counterpart, learning, as solely dependent on specific brain regions. Learning and memory are attributed to changes in neuronal synapses, thought to be mediated by long-term potentiation and long-term depression.

Hebb distinguished between short-term and long-term memory. He postulated that any memory that stayed in short-term storage for a long enough time would be consolidated into a long-term memory. Later research showed this to be false. Research has shown that direct injections of cortisol or epinephrine help the storage of recent experiences. This is also true for stimulation of the amygdala.

This proves that excitement enhances memory by the stimulation of hormones that affect the amygdala. Excessive or prolonged stress (with prolonged cortisol) may hurt memory storage.

Patients with amygdalar damage are no more likely to remember emotionally charged words than non-emotionally charged ones. The hippocampus is important for explicit memory. The hippocampus is also important for memory consolidation. The hippocampus receives input from different parts of the cortex and sends its output out to different parts of the brain also. The input comes from secondary and tertiary sensory areas that have processed the information a lot already. Hippocampal damage may also cause memory loss and problems with memory storage.

Disorders

Much of the current knowledge of memory has come from studying memory disorders. Loss of memory is known as amnesia. There are many sorts of amnesia, and by studying their different forms, it has become possible to observe apparent defects in individual sub-systems of the brain's memory systems, and thus hypothesise their function in the normally working brain.

Other neurological disorders such as Alzheimer's disease can also affect memory and cognition. Hyperthymesia, or hyperthymesic syndrome, is a disorder which affects an individual's autobiographical memory, essentially meaning that they cannot forget small details that otherwise would not be stored. Korsakoff's syndrome, also known as Korsakoff's psychosis, amnesic-confabulatory syndrome, is an organic brain disease that adversely affects memory.

While not a disorder, a common *temporary* failure of word retrieval from memory is the tip-of-the-tongue phenomenon. Sufferers of Nominal Aphasia (also called Anomia), however, do experience the tip-of-the-tongue phenomenon on an ongoing basis due to damage to the frontal and parietal lobes of the brain.

Memorisation

Memorisation is a method of learning that allows an individual to recall information verbatim. Rote learning is the method most often used.

Methods of memorising things have been the subject of much discussion over the years with some writers, such as Cosmos Rossellius using visual alphabets.

The spacing effect shows that an individual is more likely to remember a list of items when rehearsal is spaced over an extended period of time.

In contrast to this is cramming which is intensive memorisation in a short period of time. Also relevant is the Zeigarnik effect which states that people remember uncompleted or interrupted tasks better than completed ones.

In March 2007 German researchers found they could use odors to re-activate new memories in the brains of people while they slept and the volunteers remembered better later.

At the Centre for Cognitive Science at Ohio State University, researchers have found that memory accuracy of adults is hurt by the fact that they know more than children and tend to apply this knowledge when learning new information. Interference can hamper memorisation and retrieval. There is retroactive interference when learning new information causes you to forget old information and proactive interference where learning one piece of information makes it harder to learn similar new information.

Emotion can have a powerful impact on memory. Numerous studies have shown that the most vivid autobiographical memories tend to be of emotional events, which are likely to be recalled more often and with more clarity and detail than neutral events.

Improving Memory

It's inconclusive that memory may be improved via simple lifestyle changes such as undertaking memory exercises, eating healthily, engaging in moderate physical activity, and reducing stress.

The International Longevity Centre released in 2001 a report which includes recommendations for keeping the mind in good functionality until advanced age. Some of the recommendations are to stay intellectually active through learning, training or reading, to keep physically active so to promote blood circulation to the brain, to socialise, to reduce stress, to keep sleep time regular, to avoid depression or emotional instability and to observe good nutrition.

Memory Tasks

- **Paired associate learning** - When one learns to associate one specific word with another. For example when given a word such as "safe" one must learn to say another specific word, such as "green". This is stimulus and response.

- **Free recall**- During this task a subject would be asked to study a list of words and then sometime later they will be asked to recall or write down as many words that they can remember.
- **Recognition**- Subjects are asked to remember a list of words or pictures, after which point they are asked to identify the previously presented words or pictures from among a list of alternatives that were not presented in the original list.

■■■

Chapter 2

The Architecture of Memory

In Mind Development we recognise the process of memorisation has several sequential stages: Sensory Memory; Short-term Memory; Medium-term Memory; and Long-term Memory - with further sub-categories of memory described.

This understanding opens many doorways both to improved memorisation techniques and to enhanced awareness of our mental processes, and hence the possibility of meta-cognitive control.

Sensory Memory

All incoming information is held briefly (1/2 to 2 seconds) in Sensory Memory as a primitive and unanalysed copy of the actual sensory information. This storage takes place in the Primary Sensory Cortex, which is why this type of memory is so vivid and lifelike, whilst it lasts.

Auditory (hearing) information is held in 'echoic' memory. To understand echoic memory, imagine someone rattling off a string of numbers, then stopping suddenly and asking you what were the last 5 numbers he or she said. To answer the question, you would have to 'replay' what you had heard. Fortunately, the last few numbers would probably still be in your echoic memory, and most likely you could answer the question correctly. If the person had stopped and waited a few seconds before asking the question, however, probably you would not remember any of the numbers - you could not 'replay the tape.' Echoic memories fade after a few seconds.

Visual information is held is 'iconic' memory. To understand iconic memory, look around you and then shut your eyes. For a short time, you retain a vivid image of everything you just saw. However, as you try to analyse the details, the image fades very rapidly, within 1/2 of a second.

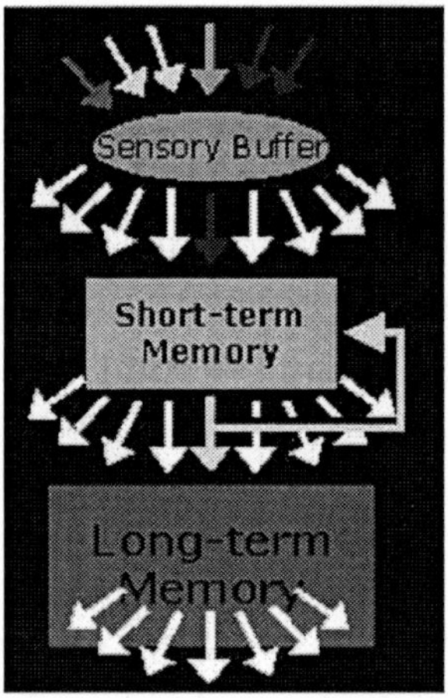

If most of the information in sensory memory fades away and does not get processed further, what determines which information is selected for further processing? Considerable evidence from research suggests that it is the information that we ***pay attention to*** that moves on for further processing.

Short-term Memory

The sensory information's next port of call is the Forebrain. It then becomes Short-term Memory. The duration of Short-term Memory depends upon the type of material being stored. Without active rehearsal, numbers are stored for 10 to 15 seconds, but colours are stored for up to 3 minutes.

When you are talking or answering questions on an exam, the information must be brought into Working Memory for you to manipulate, and your words and answers come out of Working Memory. As you try to understand the words on this page, your ability to understand these concepts depends on your Working Memory and also to some extent – when contextual information needs to be retrieved – from your Long-term Memory.

Short-term Memory is limited in terms of the both its capacity (amount of information it can hold) and its duration (length of time it can hold information). It is fluid and ever-changing – the focus of our consciousness.

Imagine that you are asked to remember a telephone number that is new to you. You could probably keep it in your memory for more than 30 seconds, but only by saying it over and over again 'in your head.' This is called 'rote rehearsal' or 'maintenance rehearsal.'

This can help you to keep information in Short-term Memory for more than 30 seconds but if anything happens to interrupt your rote rehearsal, the information will be lost, unless you have already succeeded through an effort of memorisation to move the information into Medium or Long-term Memory. You can probably think of real life examples where this has happened: you were trying to keep a telephone number in your head, but someone interrupted your thoughts and you lost the number forever.

Our Short-term Memory at any time contains the information with which we reason. Working Memory is that part of Short-term Memory that contains the information we use for thinking: visually, verbally and numerically.

The main functions of short-term memory can be itemised as follows:

1. The Articulatory Loop
2. The Visuo-Spatial Sketch Pad
3. The Central Executive
4. Episodic and Semantic Buffers

There are many other subsidiary functions but these are the ones that should be readily accessible and whose function can be improved.

Not everybody has developed this range of functions to the limit of his ability. Circumstances may have resulted in your developing one faculty at the expense of the others. Development of all these functions, some of which reside in the Left and some in the Right hemispheres of the brain, means that we have to become specialised in these areas. Lack of specialised centres in the brain is called Bicamerality (two cameras), because the functions of the left and right hemispheres are the same and duplicate each other.

This results in indecision and other problems of dual personality. Thus, there is inefficiency, not only in executive action but in the duplication of information left and right. The primary objective of the Mind Development exercises at this level is to get rid of this Bicamerality, so that your will can be united and your brain becomes a more effective instrument.

The Articulatory Loop

The function of the Articulatory Loop is to rehearse speech sub-vocally, that is silently. This is necessary in order to maintain a memory trace as an electrical vibration in the Short-term

Memory. A process of sub-vocal rehearsal is used to refresh a fading memory trace before it decays into inaccessibility. The evidence for the existence of this loop is as follows:

(a) Errors in speech often have an acoustic or phonemic similarity, for example F instead of S, B instead of G. It is harder to remember passages with similar speech sounds - the letter sequence of DBCTPG is harder to remember than KWYLRQ, test this for yourself.

(b) The effect of articulatory suppression, that is, for example, forcing someone to repeat a common word like 'the' while they are trying to remember a series of digits. This has the effect of reducing the number of digits that can be recalled, i.e. the 'digit span'.

These two factors mean that the length and accuracy of the digit span depends upon the ability to rehearse the material sub-vocally.

(c) It is easier to remember short words than long ones. Short syllable words like 'bishop' or 'rivet' are easier to remember than words with long vowel sounds like 'harpoon' or 'Friday'. Slowly spoken words are not well remembered. It has been found that digit span levels for Welsh-speaking children are less than those for English-speaking children. This is because the time required to read digits in Welsh is longer. The difference disappears when irrelevant speech sounds are used, and proves that English and Welsh speakers are intellectually equal.

Thus, one can say that the efficiency of the Articulatory Loop depends critically on the time taken to say the message, i.e. fast talkers remember better. In short, you can remember as much as you can say in 3 seconds, which is typically the length of the loop. (Our findings are that a child of 8 years speaks at 1.5 words per second and a child of 12 years speaks at 2.5 words per second. The child of 8 has a digit span of approx. 4 and the child of 12 has a digit span of about 7, so this indicates that 3 seconds is about the right figure).

If we gave you a series of letters to remember, your ability to remember the series correctly would probably depend on the number of letters in the series, which you could 'fit into' the 3 seconds of the Articulatory Loop. Most people can remember a series of letters correctly if there are only 3 or 5 letters in the series.

About half the people asked to remember a seven-letter series have difficulty. Relatively few people can remember a series consisting of 9 or 11 letters correctly. This finding, that the limit on Short-term Memory is typically around 7 items, is one of the most consistent findings in all of psychology. George Miller, a very famous cognitive psychologist, coined the phrase "the magical number seven, plus or minus two," to describe the capacity of Working Memory.

Working Memory is clearly essential if we are trying to understand a spoken sentence, or remember a string of digits. Working Memory is an active process where the goal is not necessarily to move the information into permanent storage, but to keep it available until it is put to use – think of a phone number you'll repeat to yourself until you can dial it on the phone. We essentially 'think' out of our working memory, but the capacity of Working Memory is only seven (plus or minus two) items. If the limit on working memory was literally 7 letters, we could not write our own names, much less form a complete sentence.

It is true that Short-term memory has a capacity of 7 something, but the limit is not necessarily 7 letters. We can increase the working capacity of Short-term Memory by combining bits of information into meaningful units, or chunks.

So the memory span of young adults is typically around seven elements, called chunks, regardless whether the elements are digits, letters, words, or other units. However, that span does depend on the category of chunks used (e.g., span is around seven for digits, around six for letters, and around 5 for words), and even on features of the chunks within a category.

For instance, span is lower for long than for short words. In general, memory span for verbal contents (digits, letters, words, etc.) strongly depends on the time it takes to speak the contents aloud, and on the lexical status of the contents (i.e., whether the contents are words known to the person or not).

A new piece of information may be connected by association with things that we already know or will readily be reminded of, or which are typically linked by logic or character. This connection then forms a single chunk in our symbol space. Many memorisation techniques take advantage of this to effectively expand Working Memory.

Focusing on meaning therefore helps with chunking. Understanding the meaning of information to be learned involves understanding how new information relates to other new information or to information you already know.

Focusing on meaning not only helps with chunking, it also

helps you to get information into and out of Long-term Memory in the most efficient way.

Repetition in itself is not a very efficient strategy for moving information from Short-term to Long-term Memory, but if we focus on the meaning of information to be learned and try to relate it to information that is already in our Long-term Memory, this seems to help the new information to be effectively filed away. Since Long-term Memory appears to 'file' information according to meaning, this will also help you to be able to find that information when you need quick access to it in the future.

The Articulatory Loop also appears to be a useful checking mechanism which is good at preserving the order in which information is to be given out. This is particularly noticeable when one is asked to suppress sub-vocalisation by saying a word repeatedly under your breath.

If two words of a given passage were then reversed, one would be less likely to notice whilst suppressing sub-vocalisation. Thus, one would use sub-vocalisation when reading difficult prose, e.g. a legal document where meticulously accurate comprehension is necessary.

But one might not sub-vocalise very much when reading a novel, since the concepts are easy to understand. What one does experience while reading romantic fiction, however, is a mental image of the sound of the characters speaking, as well as a visualisation of their surroundings.

These 'voices' are not the function of the Articulatory Loop, but of another system which produces auditory and visual imagery.

The Visuo-Spatial Sketch Pad

Visuo-Spatial perception refers to our ability to process and interpret visual information about where objects are in space. This is an important aspect of cognitive functioning because it is responsible for a wide range of activities of daily living. For instance, it underlies our ability to move around in an environment and orient ourselves appropriately. Visuo-Spatial perception is also involved in our ability to accurately reach for objects in our visual field and our ability to shift our gaze to different points in space.

The association areas of the visual cortex are separated into 2 major component pathways, and are believed to mediate different aspects of visual cognition. In humans, the parieto-occipital region is believed to process Visuo-Spatial and Visuo-Motor types of information, dealing with location. Whereas, the inferotemporal region of the brain is believed to mediate our ability to process visual information about the shape, colour and texture of objects. The Sketch Pad can be used, for example, for constructing and manipulating visual images, and for the representation of mental maps.

Try multiplying 8 X 13 in your head. You will find that to perform this calculation mentally you will need to 'carry' digits which have to be held over in the memory. To do this you may imagine a blackboard on which you chalk the figures; this then we can define as the Visuo-Spatial Sketch Pad. It is a specialised visualisation function of the right hemisphere.

In addition to the visualisation faculty there appears to be the ability to hold spatial recording in memory. Blind people are able to find their way about, bats can navigate in the dark by the reflections of the high-frequency sounds they emit, one can learn to touch type without seeing the keyboard.

Words which can be visualised are more easily memorised than those which cannot. It is therefore possible to use visual imagery as a mnemonic system for the purpose of remembering random sequences of numbers and words.

There is evidence that images are stored directly in the brain, which means that information can be accessed rapidly if it is linked to an image, or ideogram, and if perceived material is reduced to these ideograms.

This probably does not apply to long-term memory; for reasons of data space the images are converted into an abstract code as they would be in a computer's memory. In order to display and operate upon various images stored in Long-term Memory we need to have a recall system functioning through codes or keywords.

Once the image is recalled to Short-term Memory it can then run as a programme would in a computer, creating the image in the mind's eye and operate upon it.

The ability to visualise is reduced if the subject is asked to point to something while seeing a picture, but heavy verbal tasks, such as grammatical analysis of sentences, do not interfere with the image. If you have ever tried to form a mental picture while driving a car you will realise how dangerous this can be.

Nevertheless it is possible to hold conversations with other passengers or listen to the radio without danger. Visual imagery can also be affected by heavy demands upon one's mathematical and logical faculties. Being called upon to make a difficult decision seems to affect the area of executive control necessary to maintain the image.

Spatial memory is an essential part of our ability to function as an individual within our environment. For instance, if we were to walk into a darkened room that was very familiar to me, we would have a good idea where all the individual items in the room were so that we didn't walk into them.

In order for us to be able to do this, we need to be able to remember what is in the room and where they all are in relation to our entry point, the door. In short, we need an internal map of the room. The map consists of three elements; what items are present, where they are in relation to each other and where we are, in relation to both those items and the room in general.

The generation and operation of such maps require the integration of multiple neural systems. In order to recognise and recall what is present in the room, two neural systems come into operation. A recognition system based in the Perirhinal Cortex tells us that the items present are familiar to me. A second system that deals with the arrangements of individual items based in the Hippocampus tells us how these items are arranged in relation to each other.

The Central Executive

When a person needs to simultaneously perform mental tasks such holding and manipulating data and images, and reasoning with that information. Short-term Memory must allocate available cognitive resources. Short-term Memory is like the control tower of a major airport, responsible for scheduling and coordinating all incoming and outgoing flights.

To achieve this, there are the two 'slave systems' described above, the Articulatory Loop and the Visuo-Spatial Sketch Pad responsible for short-term maintenance of information, and a Central Executive responsible for the supervision of integrating the information and for coordinating the slave systems.

The Central Executive is, among other things, responsible for directing attention to relevant information, suppressing irrelevant information and inappropriate actions, and for coordinating cognitive processes when more than one task must be done at the same time.

Here we have a mechanism which is subject to the collective will of the individual, acting on the summation of all desires, needs, motivations and conditioning. This consensus acts as the driving force which powers the Executive and causes it to search endlessly in a closed loop around all the sensory inputs looking for information which can be used in the service of this collective will and to fulfil its aims.

It is more like a slave than a master in responding to the whole organism. Freud's concept of the Libido, which was the interaction of creative and destructive forces forms only a small part of the total influence upon the Executive, which acts upon other drives for power and guidance from the Ego and Superego.

Episodic and Semantic Buffers

Baddely has postulated a fourth component in the Working Memory, in addition to the Articulatory Loop, the Sketch Pad and the Central Executive.

There is a temporary store for information he calls the Episodic Buffer, which holds representations that integrate episodic information (concrete, experiential data) into a unitary episodic representation.

This information would include phonological, visual, and spatial information and data retrieved from Long-term Memory.

As yet, the storage location of the Episodic Buffer is not certain, but it is surmised that it may be the Hippocampus, as this would explain a lot of phenomena. In our opinion, the Episodic Buffer acts as a bridge between Short-term Working Memory and the locations of Medium-term Memory and Long-term Working Memory (readily accessible expert information).

Medium-term Memory is, for the most part, episodic and temporary, though some of its contents may be stored in Long-term memory if they need to be. Long-term Working Memory is a temporary store of expert knowledge retrieved from Long-term Memory for the task at hand – it is a very much expanded Episodic Buffer.

Recent studies have led to the proposal that Working Memory operates not as a gateway between sensory input and Long-term Memory but as a Workspace.

Access to acquired knowledge and prior learning in Medium and Long-term Memory occurs and is integrated in the Episodic Buffer with current sensory input before that complex of information becomes available to Working Memory.

Further research is supporting the existence of a Semantic Buffer, filling a similar role to the Episodic Buffer but for semantic material. The Semantic Buffer is a Working Memory centre that stores meaning(s), rather then the surface features of words and phrases.

In this way, the theme or topic of an entire discourse may be held in mind, and one may paraphrase or translate to an alternative language. In short, there is a storage buffer for the lexical context of discourse.

Current experimental work has suggested that such global structures of meaning play an important part in the cognitive processing of discourse, e.g. in comprehension and recall.

Working Memory

Working Memory is the active system that temporarily stores and manipulates information that is needed in the execution of complex cognitive tasks, such as learning, reasoning and comprehension. Working Memory is all that is currently in view.

There are two types of components: storage and central executive functions. The four storage systems within the model are the Articulatory Loop and Semantic Buffer (which are responsible for the temporary storage of verbal and semantic information respectively) and the Visuo-Spatial Sketch Pad and Episodic Buffer (which are responsible for the temporary storage of visual and sensory information).

The Central Executive is very active in Working Memory and is responsible for the selection, initiation and termination of processing routines (e.g. encoding, storing, and retrieving). Encoding refers to the processes of placing items into memory. Retrieval refers to the processes through which we recover items from memory.

The Structure of Working Memory:

The Central Executive is a limited capacity system used for a variety of purposes, including tasks that involve planning or decision making; trouble shooting in situations in which the automatic processes appear to be running into difficulty; novel situations; dangerous or technically difficult situations; and situations where strong habitual responses or temptations are involved.

Extensive damage to the frontal lobes may result in impairments in Central Executive functioning. The classic frontal syndrome is characterised by "disturbed attention, increased distractibility, a difficultly in grasping the whole of a complicated state of affairs... well able to work along old routines but cannot learn to master new types of task, in new situations."

An important function of the Working Memory is the ability to store and manipulate numbers. We can recognise similarities, like an 'And' function, we can add, subtract, multiply and divide.

Our arithmetical digit span seems to depend upon speed - the faster one can operate with the information stored in Working Memory, the greater the span and accuracy.

Until recently, a person's IQ – a measure of all kinds of mental problem-solving abilities, including spatial skills, memory and verbal reasoning – was thought to be a fixed commodity largely determined by genetics. But recent modern research demonstrates that the very basic brain function called Working Memory in fact underlies our general intelligence, in particular our Fluid Intelligence, opening up the intriguing possibility that if you improve your Working Memory, you would boost your IQ too. This is what Mind Development has found to be the case, over many years experience.

Reasoning ability is central to intelligence. Fluid Intelligence relates to our ability to solve novel problems. Although many different cognitive processes may be executed in the solution of a task, individual differences in Working Memory efficiency, skills and resources play a crucial role in determining the speed and correctness of the results obtained.

Measures of Working Memory capacity are strongly related to performance in other complex cognitive tasks such as reading comprehension and problem solving skills, and with measures of the intelligence quotient. Some researchers have argued that working memory capacity reflects the efficiency of executive functions, most notably the ability to maintain a few task-relevant representations in the face of distracting irrelevant information.

The tasks seem to reflect individual differences in ability to focus and maintain attention, particularly when other events are serving to capture attention. These effects seem to be a function of frontal brain areas.

Working Memory is the brain's short-term information storage system. It's a workbench for solving mental problems. For example if you calculate 71 - 7 + 6, your Working Memory will store the intermediate steps necessary to work out the answer. And the amount of information that the Working Memory can hold is strongly related to general intelligence.

Of course, writing things down is an important way of extending Working Memory, and this enables organisation of information and calculations to be accomplished that would not be possible for most people with information held within the mental space alone. However, using notes to extend Working Memory does not exercise and improve the mental ability to hold and juggle a large number of items in the mind, with instant random access to each, as is needed for maximum fluid intelligence.

Recent studies suggest that Working Memory can be improved by training. After training, measured brain activity related to Working Memory increased in the prefrontal cortex, an area that many researchers have associated with Working Memory functions.

Perhaps of greater importance, another study has found a period of Working Memory training increases a range of cognitive abilities and increases IQ test scores. Working Memory training – as accomplished, for example, by the memorisation techniques – is therefore key to unlocking brain power.

I-tags

Within the mind, visual experiences can be distinguished from auditory experiences and from experiences of other sensory modalities. In turn, perceptual experiences can be distinguished from memories, emotions, thoughts, etc. This universal ability implies that certain features of data coming into the field of consciousness can be consciously noted and marked or 'tagged' as such.

Tags are thus seen to form the basis both of phenomenal consciousness and the self. Recently the concept of tagging has been recognised as a fundamental aspect of the creation of memories. Brian Lancaster explains the continuity of the self by means of 'I-tags.' These are the basic data from which our sense of identity is constructed.

He proposed that when an event is consciously experienced, its representation in memory includes a reference to the 'I' which actually experienced the event. There is a personal connection and identification with the experienced perception. Subsequent voluntary recall consists of making a connection to the appropriate I-tag. When an I-tag exists there is no effort required to 'find the memory.'

At any given moment, a number of such I-tags are activated, as sensory systems interact with memory. We may intentionally evoke an I-tag or similarity of circumstances may remind us of stored I-tags.

Thus, we may be using a mouse which triggers one I-tag, sitting at our desk, which includes memories of its purchase, another I-tag, listening to favourite music, another I-tag, and so on. Each I-tag embodies our past identity state when the given entity was experienced previously. The 'I' is continually constructed from an endless flux of I-tags.

Each individual I-tag is the basis of meaning since it embodies the individual's involvement with some specific object or event in the past. It is this 'involvement' – of making an impression with the current sense of self – which makes the difference between experience passing by as a stream, and it's incorporation into our memory storage.

Unless a memory is I-tagged it cannot usually be recalled, it is filed directly into Trash files. Recall will then only occur in the presence of an appropriate environmental trigger (souvenir), or through retrieval by hypnosis. In short, we have to have an I-tag to retrieve something. Mnemonics provide, such a tag.

Medium-term Memory

From the Forebrain, the remaining material is transferred to the Hippocampus where the consolidation of the material in preparation for sending to Long-term Memory takes place. The Hippocampus is the storage site of Medium-term Memory, which is stored for 24 to 48 hours.

Medium-term Memory is a separate system, intermediating between Short-term Memory and Long-term Memory. Short-term storage is electronic, Medium-term storage is chemical and Long-term storage is protein based.

Medium-term Memory is a way station and sorting house where information is stored for a few hours up to 48 hours, in case it is useful. Most of this data is eventually classed as not useful and discarded; the remainder of this Hippocampal content is consolidated and passed on to Long-term Memory.

If we only had a Short-term Memory and a Long-term Memory, most of what we have learned would be forgotten in the first two minutes, not over a period of 48 hours or so, where it can be used and evaluated, and the most useful stored for later re-use.

Without Medium-term Memory, we would not be able to find the car in the evening that we parked in the morning, before we started work. And we would not be able to enjoy a novel, because we would have forgotten the beginning of the page long before we got to the end; we would no longer have a global grasp of the story. Many phenomena are explained by reference to Medium-term Memory.

One researcher suggests that dreams are forgotten within a minute because there is no Medium-term store, only a Short-term store, and that unless information is stored first in Medium-term Memory and reviewed several times, it will not re-file as Long-term Memory.

Note that Medium-term Memory capacity can be increased by intensive practice over a long period, for example learning the intricate maps of London if you wish to be a taxi driver, or spending 10 hours every day memorising the Koran. The Hippocampus has the capacity to grow new cells, if it is used extensively, so the size of the Hippocampus is increased in size, especially the posterior Hippocampus.

The major difference between Short-term Memory and Medium-term Memory is that Short-term Memory content is lost if we switch our attention to another task, but Medium-term Memory content is not. It is still there when we return to it - material stored at this level is stored for hours.

How long it is retained and whether it is then stored for long-term retrieval, depends on how actively we review and refer to the information.

No matter how diligently one studies, no matter how well material seems to have been learned a few minutes after completing the task, it is not long before time begins to erode our memory. An hour later, it may be possible to recall little more than half or even a quarter of what was committed to memory (and far less if no effort was made to pay attention to the material, understand its meanings and inter-relationships, and compare it to existing knowledge).

A day later, almost everything seems to have evaporated from the mind, except perhaps for the most stand-out or impressive facts. People forget what they had tried so hard to remember at a rate corresponding to the following graph:

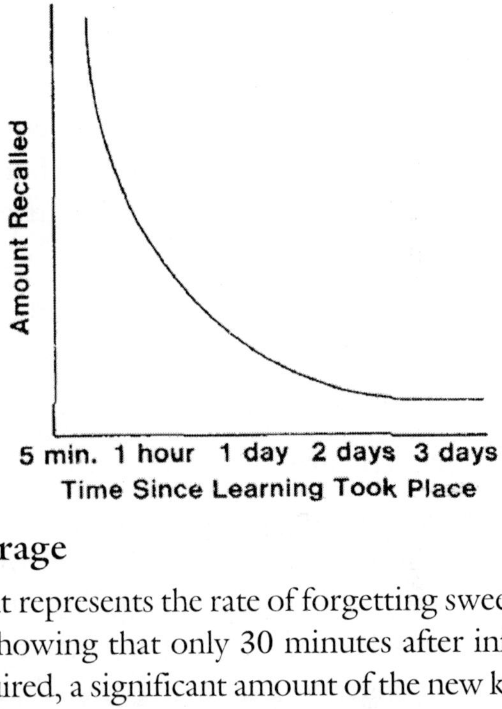

Passive Storage

The curve that represents the rate of forgetting sweeps swiftly downward, showing that only 30 minutes after information has been acquired, a significant amount of the new knowledge is already being lost. For the first 30 minutes, a lot of what we have learned may be retrieved from Medium-term Memory, but after about 30 minutes, the first stage of consolidation begins so the rate of forgetting becomes rapid.

Memory continues to suffer a rapid decline and after 4 hours about 50% of the content has been forgotten, and 90% has been forgotten after 24 hours - or even less if the material had not been properly paid attention to in the first place. Which means we retain at most about 10 percent of the information we hoped to commit to memory - *unless* a more active process of remembering is adopted.

Active Storage

Material that is rehearsed, because we are actively working on it (e.g. using the information at work) will be reliably stored for several hours and some residue will remain for several days.

In the case of Active Storage, approximately 20% to 30% of the material being worked on is transferred to Long-term Memory. It is impossible to give an exact figure; this depends on how impressionable is the data – its relative importance and emotional colouring.

Even more effective is a regular schedule of review, incorporating key words and key images, to retain 50% or more of the information.

Mnemonic Storage

When Mnemonics using powerful associations and images are made, Medium-term Memory is 100% reliable for about 4 to 6 hours and about 90% reliable after 24 hours, if there has been no rehearsal of the encoded material. If material is to be available for a longer period and to be 100% accurate, rehearsal must take place.

Unless the material in Medium-term Memory is rehearsed or reviewed several times it will eventually be forgotten. In contrast, if Mnemonics have been used in conjunction with rehearsal – i.e. the information has been recalled, reviewed, actively used, thought about and integrated - most, if not all, of this encoded material is transferred to Long-term Memory, in which case recall is nearly 100% even after several years.

Mnemonics enhance Medium-term Memory, so unless the material that has been recoded in mnemonic form is reviewed three or four times it will, for the most part, be forgotten.

Mnemonics enhance our capacity to duplicate; once we have duplicated a passage or whatever, we can play with it mentally. This mental play, a combination of comparing and contrasting will lead to understanding and once the material is understood it will become part of Permanent Memory.

Our potential for memorisation is much greater than our usual practical ability. When the time of exposure to the source material and the time of recall is after only a short delay our recall of the material is almost as great as our full potential, but the gap starts to widen rapidly after as little as half an hour.

With suitable prompts, most of the material could be recovered from potential Medium-term Memory even after several days, although not much longer than that, because true forgetfulness has started to occur – much of the material in Medium-term Memory is erased after a few days. This is why our recognition span is so good.

When we recognise something the thing itself is the prompt. Mnemonics are a special kind of prompt. When we use the formal mnemonic systems to encode material, this material can be recovered even after several days, because the mnemonics act as a series of recognition prompts so the original memory is retrieved. Key Words behave in a similar manner; Key Words act as prompts or triggers, so the original wording of the passage can be retrieved from potential memory.

Why use Mnemonics if, by and large, storage is at the level of the Medium-term Memory and forgetfulness will occur in three or four days? When used correctly Mnemonics can reduce learning time to about a third.

To give you an example, there are forty and some American Presidents since the time of George Washington. Without Mnemonics you would have to rehearse this list of Presidents about 100 times to make a permanent memory. Learning the same list in conjunction with mnemonics would probably take less than half an hour. A memory expert could do something similar in about ten minutes.

Okay, you may say, but we will forget this list in about three or four days, because this material is not actually in Long-term Memory. This is true unless you use rehearsal and connection of the information with your wider knowledge base. If the material is already in Medium-term Memory, however, you will only have to review it about four to six times to make the memory permanent, so there is a considerable saving in the time taken to learn the list and make it part of Permanent Memory.

Unless you are using mnemonics there is a bottleneck between Short-term Memory and Medium-term Memory: many repetitions are required to get the information into Medium-term Memory. Mnemonics allow a person to overcome this.

Once material is in Medium-term Memory you will have an illusion that you have learned it; this is not true, it will be forgotten in a few days at most, very little will have entered Long-term Memory. To transfer material from Medium-term Memory to Long-term Memory involves over-learning: it must be repeated several times to make it important enough to transfer to Long-term Memory and integrated with the existing knowledge base.

The important dimension in Medium-term Memory is how many times have you recalled the material in a meaningful context, not just the number of times you have been exposed to it. If something is recalled several times it becomes sufficiently important to be stored in Long-term Memory.

Many students cram just before an exam. When they do this, they only have the material stored at the level of Medium-term Memory. They believe they have learned the material, but they forget what they have crammed soon after the examination.

Mnemonics should not replace understanding unless you are doing party tricks, otherwise there will be little storage in Long-term Memory. Long-term Memory operates best with meaningful material.

Semantic and Episodic Memory

Material in Medium-term Memory is sorted into three categories: Semantic Memory (meaningful information and concepts), Episodic Memory (episodes of life experience) and Trash.

The Trash memory is forgotten as far as the conscious mind is concerned, although some of this content may continue to be stored in Implicit long-term storage and have subconscious effects. It may possibly be retrieved by a hypnotist and is the basis for Recognition memory..

Medium-term Memory is sometimes called Transient

Episodic Memory in the literature; this is in fact a good definition, because Medium-term Memory has high imagery content, whereas, in contrast, Permanent Memory or Long-term Memory proper has a large Semantic (conceptual) dimension.

For example, if you were to go to a lecture, then recall it in the bus on the way home, in most cases this recall would be accompanied by imagery of the lecture, whereas if you were to try to recall the lecture a month later, for the most part your recall would be Semantic: most of the perceptual details will have been forgotten.

Contrary to popular belief much of our autobiographical memory is Semantic; we tend to create imagery after the fact, little perceptual imagery is the original perceptions. One exception for many people, however, is the auditory imagery of music. Songs and music, in common with Episodic memory, are stored in the right hemisphere, whereas Semantic memories are stored in the left.

Until the age of about 14, Episodic Memory (memory for events) is predominant. From the age of 14, Semantic Memory (memory for information) starts to play a larger role and by the age of 18 at the latest, Semantic Memory plays the predominant role.

During childhood the right hemisphere dominates in most case, but after the age of 18 the left hemisphere is the dominant hemisphere for 90% of the population.

Most adults may have a good recall of events of the last couple of days, because most of the content of Medium-term Memory is Episodic, but they will tend to have a poor recall of events from last week or last year, because they tend to rely on longer-term Semantic Memory stored in the left hemisphere.

They may know that they went to Brighton the week before and they may know they went by train, because this is the usual way to get to Brighton, but they may have little or no memory of the train journey itself, because they are using the more abstract Semantic Memory to reconstruct the episode of going to Brighton, instead of getting in the right-brain mode to relive the experience.

In terms of general intelligence, researchers often differentiate between fluid and crystallised intelligence. **Fluid intelligence** relates to our ability to solve novel problems and is intrinsic to the functioning of Working Memory.

Crystallised intelligence, on the other hand, refers to our accumulated knowledge and experiences and how well we can access and use these, as well as practical intelligence, or the ability to solve to deal with everyday problems and situations. Semantic Memory stored in the left hemisphere is the basis of Crystallised intelligence. Fluid intelligence tends to be negatively affected by age, although this varies among individuals.

Crystallised intelligence is generally well preserved and may even improve in some areas in old age, which supports the idea that wisdom comes with age and experience. In our opinion, increases in Crystallised intelligence across the life-span more than compensate for the decrements in Fluid intelligence that occurs after the age of forty. The secret of making large increases in Crystallised intelligence is to continue to study until we are on our death bed!

Long-term Memory

The brain needs to organise complex information in Working Memory before it can be encoded into Long-term Memory. In this process of organisation, the meaningfulness or emotional content of an item may play a role in its retention into Long-term Memory. If it is considered important, the information will remain in Medium-term Memory, particularly if one has used memorisation techniques such as chunking or mnemonics.

The process of further consolidation in Medium-term Memory starts after about 30 minutes. From the Hippocampus, the selected memories are passed on to the Parietal Lobes. Semantic Memory to the Left Parietal Lobe and Episodic to the Right Parietal Lobe.

During our waking hours some information can be transferred from the Hippocampus to the Parietal Lobes (the first stage of consolidation), but there is little or no transfer from the Parietal Lobes to the Temporal Lobes of the Cortex during the waking state. Further transfer to the Temporal Lobes occurs during sleep. The Temporal Lobes are the true site of Long-term Memory.

When material is stored in Long-term Memory, the rate of forgetting drastically slows down; it is as though the information is no longer fluid but has become crystallised. Perhaps 10% of the content is lost in a year and many memories endure for a lifetime. It is the basis of our knowledge base.

For the most part, transfer from the Hippocampus to the Cortex occurs during sleep, and particularly the REM periods. Zhang proposed that sleep has two different stages: NREM (non-rapid-eye-movement) sleep for processing the Declarative (conscious, recallable) memory, and REM sleep for processing the Implicit (subconscious, unrecallable) memories. He further suggested that there are two types of dreams.

The type we dream, a thought-like dream, is the result of the memory replay when the Declarative memory is transferred from the Medium-term Memory to the Long-term Memory during NREM sleep. The type II dream, a more 'dream-like' dream, mainly occurs when the Implicit, subconscious memories are transferred from the Medium-term Memory to the Long-term Memory during REM sleep.

The capacity of the Hippocampus is finite, it can only store a few days experience at most. Sleep deprivation for as little as four nights is enough to turn some people insane and eight days deprivation will turn most people insane. In addition, recent studies provide compelling evidence that the Amygdala is critically involved in modulating the consolidation of Long-term memories, and particularly of emotional experiences.

Long-term Memory stores our knowledge about the world. This in turn affects our perceptions of the world, and influences what information in the environment we attend to. Long-term Memory provides the framework to which we attach new knowledge – it allows retrieval of information decades after it is stored, and it appears to be essentially unlimited in its capacity.

Schemas are mental models of the world. Psychologists believe that information in Long-term Memory is stored in large, interrelated networks of these schemas, which form intricate a knowledge network.

Related schemas are linked together, and information that activates one schema also activates ones that are closely linked. This allows relevant knowledge to be called up when information is presented.

Long-term Memory influences what aspects of a situation we pay attention to, allowing us to focus on relevant information and disregard what is not important, which allows our senses to function efficiently.

Long-term Memory may be divided into Permanent Memory and Long-term Working Memory. Permanent Memory stores information for up to a lifetime. Once material is in Permanent Memory the rate of forgetting is negligible.

It is beneficial for memorisation to connect the items to be remembered to other related information (e.g., elaborating on sentences to be remembered, mnemonic systems, or rhyming). In studying new materials it is best to:

1. Preview the material
2. Make up questions that you will look for answers to
3. Read, trying to answer the questions
4. Reflect while you read. Think of examples; relate it to what you know.
5. Recite or write a synopsis of the information in each section after you've read it. Re-read what you can't recall.
6. Review the major points and the answers to your questions at the end.

In other words, the few minutes that it takes for you to review and think about what you are trying to learn is the minimum length of time that is necessary to allow thought to become a lasting, more easily retrievable memory.

Reading, observing and listening are good methods for absorbing data and information into Working Memory. However, this information does not instantly become knowledge once we have absorbed it since it has not been encoded for long-term storage.

It can easily become forgotten if it is not accessed for some time or if new information, using the same stimuli and associations, replaces the old. To help make it part of one's permanent knowledge base, one needs to take it through a 'learning cycle' which may include:

- Comprehending and reflecting.
- Forming concepts (models, frameworks, generalisations).
- Fitting it in with previous experience and knowledge.
- Testing in new situations.
- Gaining experience in application.

Recent research has demonstrated that 7-10% of what we study is typically retained in Long-term Memory, subject to it being studied with attention and interest, but this figure may be increased greatly if mnemonics and other aids to memory such as periodic revision are utilised.

The speed of recall of information from Long-term Memory depends in part on how recently that information has been activated and it also depends on the amount of practice, i.e. the frequency and durations of reviews. A well known psychologist and researcher, Ebbinghaus, has reported that each additional recitation (after you have become familiar with the material) engraves the mental trace deeper and deeper, thus establishing a base for long-term retention.

For many people over-learning is difficult to practice because, by the time they achieve bare mastery, there is little time left and they are eager to drop the subject and go on to something else. But reciting the material even just one more time significantly increases retention, so try to remember this and utilise the technique when you can.

Long-term Working Memory

In unskilled people the Working Memory is a function of Short-term Memory and as such it is domain general. Long-term Memory may also impact on Working Memory in a domain-specific manner. In the case of experts such as mathematicians, chess masters, physicists and people of that type, part of the Long-term Memory has been recruited to create a virtual centre that we call Long-term Working Memory. By and large, this type of working memory is domain specific; in short it has a limited range of transfer.

In contrast to the Short-term Working Memory we cannot view the content all at once. We have an attention window that permits us to perceive 6-10 items or chunks at the same time. The Long-term Working Memory is like a spreadsheet and the window of attention is a parasitic function of the Short-term Working Memory.

Long-term Working Memory is a faculty enjoyed by experts in many fields. Long-term Working Memory vastly increases the expert's symbol field. It comes into being because the Forebrain parasites on the Parietal Lobes, thus the capacity of Short-term Memory are enhanced.

This is so, because Long-term Working Memory uses a relevant, fast access area of Long-term Memory. The capacity of Long-term Working Memory may be vast, but it is domain specific. There is little transfer to related skills, such as typing and playing the piano; or from playing chess to playing dominoes.

An expert in a given domain of activity, such as medicine, chess, music or golf, is "one, who has acquired special skill in or knowledge about a particular subject through professional training and practical experience". Experts will therefore, by definition, have a greater body of knowledge about their domain of expertise than other individuals.

More remarkable is the expert's accurate memory for new experiences in his or her domain. An elite athlete can, after a sports event, discuss the play-by-play action. Expert chess players can readily recall details of chess positions from their matches in recent tournaments.

Early in the twentieth century it was believed that experts were innately talented with a superior ability to store information in memory. Numerous anecdotes were collected as evidence of an unusual ability to store presented information rapidly. For example, Mozart was supposed to be able to reproduce a presented piece of music after hearing it a single time.

However, more recent research has rejected the hypothesis of a generally superior memory in experts and has demonstrated that their superior memory is limited to their domains of expertise and can be viewed as the result of acquired skills and knowledge relevant to each specific domain. Although, experienced chess players are better at remembering the positions of the balls on a pool table than novices, so there is a small measure of transfer to related tasks.

The key seems to be the use of mnemonic devices and other methods of imposing some sort of order or meaning on the information involved, such as chunking or grouping into patterns and hierarchies. To illustrate, a chess master can usually recall the positions of all the pieces on a chessboard after a quick glance.

But if the chessmen are arranged randomly and meaninglessly, his memory is reduced to near-normal. The gist is that long practice and the application of mnemonic devices can vastly improve anyone's memory and, in consequence, memory prodigies are not really so anomalous.

The Peg System of mnemonics, for example, has much in common with the Long-term Working Memory system. Material encoded on Pegs is invulnerable to distraction; it may be stored and retrieved, after several hours, with random access and 100% accuracy. A Peg System, such as the Major System or the Memory Graph, opens up the possibility of reflecting on a hundred or more ideas, rather than the three to five that you can reflect on in Short-term Working Memory. When Pegs are combined with Short Chains, to make a network of data encoded into mnemonics, their potential for advanced thinking is almost limitless.

Note: Short-term Working Memory can import ideas (data), three to five at a time, from the Peg System and, in turn, the Short-term Working Memory can export ideas (data), one by one, to the Peg System.

Long-term Working Memory is developed as a virtual centre by mnemonics experts. Although Long-term Working Memory is domain specific – a memory expert only has a Long-term Working Memory for mnemonics – the application of mnemonics is more or less domain-general, so a mnemonics expert gets the best of both worlds.

Intuition is not based on Long-term Working Memory. With Intuition, you are tapping some sub-cognitive area of the brain, possibly the cerebellum, in which case, you do not know that you know until the answer to your query becomes visible: then you know.

In the case of Long-term Working Memory, you know already that you know. You know that you have certain items in store, and that you could retrieve them if you wished, and you also know that certain items are not in store, so you can't, in which case, you know you don't know.

This is Metacognition. The only content you can actually see is the part that has been imported into Short-term Memory. At a maximum, only about nine items of data or perhaps two or three patterns can be imported into Short-term Memory from Long-term Memory at any one time. Not only do you know what is being stored in Long-term Working Memory, at any given time, you know, also, where to find any particular item, so you can import any item or collection of items into Short-term Memory, within Short-term Memory capacity limitations. Once these items have been imported into Short-term Memory – but not before – they become visible.

To draw an analogy, Long-term Working Memory is like a spread-sheet, only part of which is visible at any one time. It is like looking at the spread-sheet through the centre of a toilet roll.

If you wish to see another area, you have to shift the toilet roll, then you cannot see the area that you were looking at before, but you know it is there and you can return to it any time you want. This is the introspective experience.

In our opinion, little or nothing can be transferred to Long-term Memory in the waking state, but material from Long-term Memory can be retrieved in the waking state, and recalled rapidly when the subject has an expert memory in a specific domain of knowledge; so the storage site of Long-term Working Memory cannot be a department of Long-term Memory, if the content is to be recalled after a short period: it must be stored in Medium-term Memory.

Long-term Working Memory can only store information for a day or two, so it has much more in common with Medium-term Memory than Long-term Memory proper; like Medium-term Memory it functions through the Hippocampus and the Parietal Lobes. The Medium-term Memory acts as a mixing pot: material from Long-term Memory is contrasted and compared with information from Short-term Memory.

Contrary to some popular views, Long-term Working Memory is not infinite in its capacity. We imagine that it has the capacity to store something in the region of 50 items.

Although it has a greater storage capacity than Short-term Working Memory, it is very rigid and the speed of access is only about half of that of Short-term Memory.

There are also certain things that Long-term Working Memory cannot do, that Short-term Working Memory can.

Content can only be manipulated once it has been transferred from Long-term Working Memory to Short. From our introspective experience, the Long-term Working Memory stores patterns, rather than words and images. Words and images are constructed after the fact.

What one starts with is a sense of knowing. If what it has to show you cannot be put into some meaningful pattern, it will not be available for recall.

Because the capacity of Long-term Working Memory is tied to the recall of accepted and meaningful patterns, it does not much amplify the capacity for creative thinking.

On the other hand, Short-term Working Memory is not subject to these limitations, so anything that can extend the capacity of Short-term Memory must amplify the capacity both for reasoning and for creative thought.

How long does it take to gain a Long-term Working Memory? This depends on the domain in question. In the case of a very narrow domain, such as understanding and remembering the weather forecast, this may only take a few weeks.

Most intelligent people can already do this, so they already have a Long-term Working Memory for weather forecasts. But in the case of broad domains, such as becoming an architect, a bishop or a research chemist – or indeed, the meteorologist who prepares weather forecasts – it could take five to ten years.

It all depends on the breadth of the domain and the frequency with which Long-term Memory is accessed in that domain, integrated and used constructively, alongside Short-term Memory in the Working Memory.

Several different types of memory are included in Long-term Memory. One way to divide up Long-term Memory is into Explicit memory and Implicit memory.

Explicit Memory

Explicit memories are memories that we can consciously remember or 'declare' – they are declarative and can readily be restored to Working Memory, i.e. they are consciously available. Most of what we commonly consider 'memory' is explicit memory. Answers you give on an exam are a product of explicit memory. Everything you 'know' you remember is explicit memory.

Episodic and semantic memories are explicit. *Episodic memories* (stored in right brain for the most part) are personal, autobiographic memories of experience, such as what your first day of school was like, or what you did on your last vacation – it is memory for specific events in time, and may include emotional and multi-sensory data. Medium-term Memory may also be called, Temporary Episodic Memory.

Semantic memories (stored in left brain for the most part) are facts or meanings, such as names and dates or ideas and concepts. They are fast changing: quick to acquire but also quickly to be lost, if unused for a period of time.

Semantic Memory is, by and large a product of a literate culture, thus of recent evolutionary origin, whereas in contrast the other types of memory have an evolutionary history of millions of years.

Implicit Memory

Implicit memories are non-declarative - memories that we do

not consciously remember, which nonetheless can be show to influence our behaviour. For example, the process of conditioning. You may have been exposed to many adverts of a particular brand and taken little notice, but when visiting a supermarket, this exposure may affect your purchasing decision. This is an example of memories that we are not aware of influencing our daily behaviour as a result of conditioning.

The Implicit memory system is common to all vertebrates and accounts for associative learning; the Explicit memory system is unique to humans and requires language. The association between a subject and a predicate in language is structurally different from the associations that animals are capable of. Animals can learn associations between stimuli, but cannot infer subject-predicate associations, and that is the prerequisite to acquiring a language.

Language allows humans to think in terms of "representations", of "aboutness". Animals, who are not endowed with language, cannot grasp this "aboutness". The "aboutness" relationship is the fundamental grammatical requirement for language.

Implicit Memory is much larger than Explicit or Declarative Memory. These are further examples of Implicit Memory.

Procedural Memory represents motor or skill learning, which is memory without verbal mediation. This type of memory is encoded and probably stored by the cerebellum. It includes learning how to drive a car or tie your shoelace. Such memories are slow to acquire but more resistant to change or loss. Initial storage of Procedural Memory may be in the motor cortex and there is evidence that this storage may last for up to half an hour. The maximum rate of forgetting takes place during this period. Finally, the memory content is transferred from the motor cortex to the cerebellum. When the content has been over-learned it may be stored for a lifetime. One never forgets how to ride a bike.

Remote Memory simply refers to memories that were acquired early on. Since early acquired information is the foundation for new memories and may be linked to many further more recent memories, such memory is less subject to change and/or loss. We have little or no conscious memory of events before the age of two.

During the sensory-motor phase of development, between shortly after birth and the age of about two, memory is almost entirely procedural, hence the site of memory storage at that age is the cerebellum. This is why most traumatic material is also stored in the cerebellum: most traumatic events occur before the age of two.

Trash Memories contain information of an episodic nature that was held and used in Working Memory but not noticed significantly enough to tag it for long-term storage. It is not lost, as may appear to be the case, but is passed on to the Implicit storage of Long-term Memory. It is the basis for Recognition Memory.

The Trash file content is not open to introspection except under special circumstances, such as external triggers (e.g. a diary entry, a photograph, hypnosis or deep psychoanalysis) but it has a vast if not unlimited capacity. In addition to the Declarative and Procedural memory systems, the Trashfile/ Recognition Memory system represents a third route to Long-term Memory.

Memory can be categorised in many different ways. One such way to look at your new memories is in terms of recognition and recall (or declarative) memory. These two types of memory simply represent the depth with which you remember the new material. *Recognition memory is a superficial memory* – if you have this type of memory for a concept, you will recognise the concept when you encounter it and may be able to generate some of the material on your own if you are prompted or given clues. *Recall memory is a much deeper level of memory*. If you have this type of memory for a concept, you should be able to generate the concept at any time, without any prompting or clues.

Recognition Memory takes effect because of the large implicit recorded memory storage that cannot be recalled voluntarily, but with the correct stimulus it becomes available. This process is called Priming. People can recognise the faces of people shown in pictures if they have seen them before, even if they were long 'forgotten.'

When there is an appropriate trigger, implicit recall may be strong enough to break into conscious awareness and take on the character of Explicit Memory.

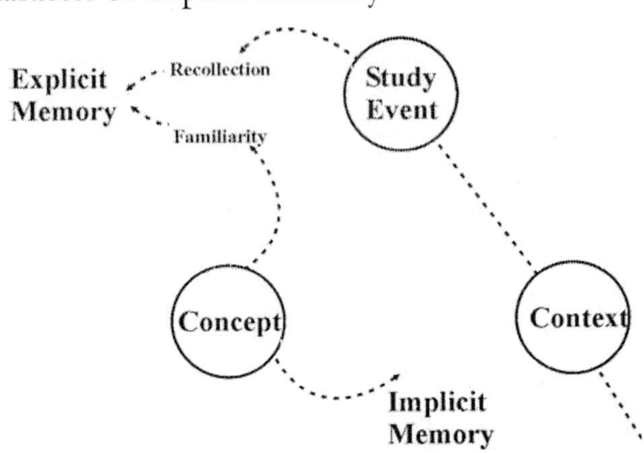

Recognition memory can be a trap. This can occur in the area of study among other things. When you come to revise some materials, often you will recognise what you are reading and think that you already know it when actually you do not. The truth is you do not know it and would not be able to answer questions about it, because the information has not been sufficiently deeply processed for encoding to Long-term Memory to have occurred.

To end on a positive note: without recognition memory life would be extremely difficult, as much of what we do depends upon it. Recollection, as defined by memory specialists, is the ability to call up specific details about an encounter when one is reminded about it, while familiarity simply knows that someone or something has been encountered before. Both are elements of recognition memory and both, new research suggests, are functions of the brain's Perirhinal Cortex. You won't run out of space because that organ is estimated to have a capacity of at least 100 billion images!

■■■

CHAPTER 3

Emotion and Memory

Emotion can have a powerful impact on memory. Numerous studies have shown that the most vivid autobiographical memories tend to be of emotional events, which are likely to be recalled more often and with more clarity and detail than neutral events. The activity of emotionally enhanced memory retention can be linked to human evolution; during early development, responsive behaviour to environmental events would have progressed as a process of trial and error. Survival depended on behavioural patterns that were repeated or reinforced through life and death situations.

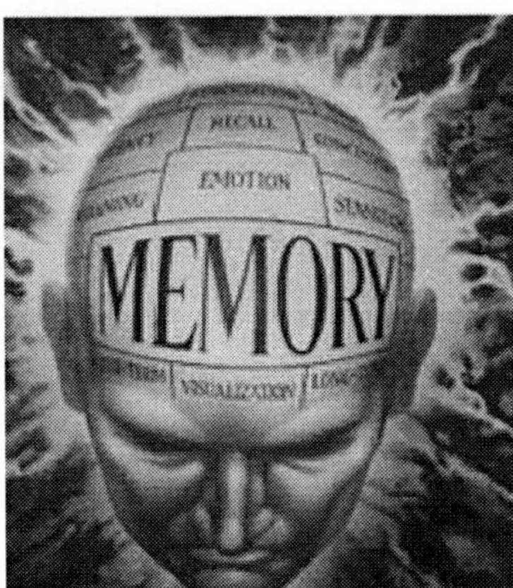

Through evolution, this process of learning became genetically embedded in humans and all animal species in what is known as "fight or flight" instinct.

Artificially inducing this instinct through traumatic physical or emotional stimuli essentially creates the same physiological condition that heightens memory retention by exciting neurochemical activity affecting areas of the brain responsible for encoding and recalling memory. This memory-enhancing effect of emotion has been demonstrated in a large number of laboratory studies, using stimuli ranging from words to pictures to narrated slide shows, as well as autobiographical memory studies. However, as described below, emotion does not always enhance memory.

Emotional Arousal and Memory

One of the most common frameworks in the emotions field proposes that affective experiences are best characterised by two main dimensions: arousal and valence. The dimension of valence ranges from highly positive to highly negative, whereas the dimension of arousal ranges from calming or soothing to exciting or agitating. Most studies so far focused on the arousal dimension of emotion as the critical factor contributing to the emotional enhancement effect on memory.

Different explanations have been offered for this effect, according to the different stages of memory formation and reconstruction.

Emotional Arousal and Encoding

From an information processing perspective, encoding refers to the process of interpreting incoming stimuli and combining the processed information.

At the encoding level the following mechanisms have been suggested as mediators of emotion effects on memory.

Selectivity of Attention

Easterbrook's cue utilisation theory predicted that high levels of arousal will lead to attention narrowing, defined as a decrease in the range of cues from the stimulus and its environment to which the organism is sensitive.

According to this hypothesis, attention will be focused primarily on the arousing details (cues) of the stimulus, so that information central to the source of the emotional arousal will be encoded while peripheral details will not. Accordingly, several studies have demonstrated that the presentation of emotionally arousing stimuli (compared to neutral stimuli) results in enhanced memory for central details (details central to the appearance or meaning of the emotional stimuli) and impaired memory for peripheral details.

Also consistent with this hypothesis are findings of weapon focus effect , in which witnesses to a crime remember the gun or knife in great detail but not other details such as the perpetrator's clothing or vehicle.

In laboratory replications it was found that participants spend a disproportionate amount of time looking at a weapon in a scene, and this looking time is inversely related to the likelihood that individuals will subsequently identify the perpetrator of the crime.

Other researchers have suggested arousal may also increase the duration of attentional focusing on the arousing stimuli, thus delaying the disengagement of attention from it. Ochsner summarised the different findings and suggested that by influencing attention selectivity and dwell time, arousing stimuli are more distinctively encoded, resulting in more accurate memory of those stimuli.

Prioritised Processing

Emotional items also appear more likely to be processed when attention is limited, suggesting a facilitated or prioritised processing of emotional information. This effect was demonstrated using the attentional blink paradigm in which two target items are presented in close temporal proximity within a stream of rapidly presented stimuli.

The typical finding is that participants often miss the second target item, as if there were a "blink" of attention following the first target's presentation, reducing the likelihood that the second target stimulus is attended.

However, when the second target stimulus elicits emotional arousal (a "taboo" word), participants are less likely to miss the target's presentation, which suggests that under conditions of limited attention, arousing items are more likely to be processed than neutral items.

Additional support for the Prioritised processing hypothesis was provided by studies investigating the visual extinction deficit.

People suffering from this deficit can perceive a single stimulus in either side visual field if it is presented alone but are unaware of the same stimulus in the visual field opposed to the lesional side, if another stimulus is presented simultaneously on the lesional side.

Emotion has been found to modulate the magnitude of the visual extinction deficit, so that items that signal emotional relevance (e.g., spiders) are more likely to be processed in the presence of competing distracters than none motional items (e.g., flowers).

Emotional Arousal and Memory Storage

In addition to its effects during the encoding phase, emotional arousal appears to increase the likelihood of memory consolidation during the retention (storage) stage of memory (the process of creating a permanent record of the encoded information). A number of studies show that over time, memories for neutral stimuli decrease but memories for arousing stimuli remain the same or improve.

Others have discovered that memory enhancements for emotional information tend to be greater after longer delays than after relatively short ones.

This delayed effect is consistent with the proposal that emotionally arousing memories are more likely to be converted into a relatively permanent trace, whereas memories for non-arousing events are more vulnerable to disruption.

A few studies have even found that emotionally arousing stimuli enhance memory **only** after a delay. The most famous of these was a study by Kleinsmith and Kaplan that found an advantage for numbers paired with arousing words over those paired with neutral words only at delayed test, but not at immediate test.

As outlined by Mather, the Kleinsmith and Kaplan effects were most likely due to a methodological confound. However, Sharot and Phelps found better recognition of arousing words over neutral words at a delayed test but not at an immediate test, supporting the notion that there is enhanced memory consolidation for arousing stimuli.

According to these theories, different physiological systems, including those involved in the discharge of hormones believed to affect memory consolidation, become active during, and closely following, the occurrence of arousing events.

Another possible explanation for the findings of the emotional arousal delayed effect is post-event processing regarding the cause of the arousal. According to the post-stimulus elaboration (PSE) hypothesis, an arousing emotional experience may cause more effort to be invested in elaboration of the experience, which would subsequently be processed at a deeper level than a neutral experience.

Elaboration refers to the process of establishing links between newly encountered information and previously stored information. It has long been known that when individuals process items in an elaborative fashion, such that meaning is extracted from items and inter-item associations are formed, memory is enhanced.

Thus, if a person gives more thought to central details in an arousing event, memory for such information is likely to be enhanced. However, these processes could also disrupt consolidation of memories for peripheral details.

Christianson suggested that the combined action of perceptual, attentional, and elaborative processing, triggered by an emotionally arousing experience, produces memory enhancements of details related to the emotion laden stimulus, at the cost of less elaboration and consolidation of memory for the peripheral details.

Emotional Valence and Memory

Even though the majority of studies have focused on the arousal dimension, a growing body of research is dedicated to the emotional valence dimension and its effects on memory. It has been claimed that this is an essential step towards a more complete understanding of emotion effects on memory. The studies that did investigate this dimension, have found that emotional valence alone can enhance memory, that is, non-arousing items with positive or negative valence can be better remembered than neutral items.

Emotional Valence and Elaboration

The processes involved in this enhancement may be distinct from those mediating the enhanced memory for arousing items. It has been suggested that in contrast to the relatively automatic attentional modulation of memory for arousing information, memory for non-arousing positive or negative stimuli may benefit instead from conscious encoding strategies, such as elaboration.

This elaborative processing can be autobiographical or semantic. Autobiographical elaboration is known to benefit memory by creating links between the processed stimuli, and the self, for example, deciding whether a word would describe the personal self.

Memory formed through autobiographical elaboration is enhanced as compared to items processed for meaning, but not in relation to the self.

Since words such as "sorrow" or "comfort" may be more likely to be associated with autobiographical experiences or self-introspection than neutral words such as "shadow", autobiographical elaboration may explain the memory enhancement of non-arousing positive or negative items.

Studies have shown that dividing attention at encoding decreases an individual's ability to utilise controlled encoding processes, such as autobiographical or semantic elaboration.

Thus, findings that participants' memory for negative non-arousing words suffers with divided attention, and that the memory advantage for negative, non-arousing words can be eliminated when participants encode items while simultaneously performing a secondary task, has supported the elaborative processing hypothesis as the mechanism responsible for memory enhancement for negative non-arousing words.

Contextual Effects of Emotion on Memory

Contextual effects occur as a result of the degree of similarity between the encoding context and the retrieval context of an emotional dimension. The main findings are that the current mood we are in affects what is attended, encoded and ultimately retrieved, as reflected in two similar but subtly different effects: the mood congruence effect and mood-state dependent retrieval.

The Mood Congruence Effect

The mood congruence effect refers to the tendency of individuals to retrieve information more easily when it has the same emotional content as their current emotional state. For instance, being in a depressed mood increases the tendency to remember negative events. This effect has been demonstrated for explicit retrieval as well as implicit retrieval.

Mood-state Dependent Retrieval

Another documented phenomenon is the mood-state dependent retrieval. The retrieval of information is more effective when the emotional state at the time of retrieval is similar to the emotional state at the time of encoding.

Thus, the probability of remembering an event can be enhanced by evoking the emotional state experienced during its initial processing. These two phenomena, the mood congruity effect and mood-state dependent retrieval, are similar to the context effects which have been traditionally observed in memory research. It may also relate to the phenomena of state-dependent memory in neuropsychopharmacology.

Thematic *vs.* Sudden Appearance of Emotional Stimuli

A somewhat different contextual effect stemmed from the recently made distinction between thematical and sudden appearance of an emotionally arousing event, suggesting that the occurrence of memory impairments depends on the way the emotional stimuli are induced.

Laney *et al.* argued that when arousal is induced thematically (i.e., not through the sudden appearance of a discrete shocking stimulus such as a weapon but rather through involvement in an unfolding event plot and empathy with the victim as his or her plight becomes increasingly apparent), memory enhancements of details central to the emotional stimulus need not come at the expense of memory impairment of peripheral details.

Laney *et al.* demonstrated this by using an audio narrative to give the presented slides either neutral or emotional meaning, instead of presenting shockingly salient visual stimuli.

In one of the experiments, participants in both the neutral

and emotional conditions viewed slides of a date scenario of a woman and man at a dinner date.

The couple engaged in conversation, then, at the end of the evening, embraced. The event concluded with the man leaving and the woman phoning a friend. The accompanying audio recording informed participants in the neutral condition that the date went reasonably well, while participants in the emotional condition heard that, as the evening wore on, the man displayed some increasingly unpleasant traits of a type that was derogatory to women, and the embrace at the end of the evening was described as an attempt to sexually assault the woman.

As expected, the results revealed that details central to the event were remembered more accurately when that event was emotional than when neutral, However, this was not at the expense of memory for peripheral (in this case, spatially peripheral or plot-irrelevant) details, which were also remembered more accurately when the event was emotional.

Based on these findings it has been suggested that the dual enhancing and impairing effects on memory are not an inevitable consequence of emotional arousal.

Memory of Felt Emotion

Many researchers use self report measures of felt emotion as a manipulation check. This raises an interesting question and a possible methodological weakness: are people always accurate when they recall how they felt in the past?

Several findings suggest this is not the case. For instance, in a study of memory for emotions in supporters of former

US presidential candidate, supporters were asked to describe their initial emotional reactions after the candidate unexpected withdrawal.

Between the assessment period, the views of many supporters changed dramatically. The results showed that supporters recalled their past emotions as having been more consistent with their current appraisals of that candidate than they actually were.

Another study found that people's memories for how distressed they felt when they learned of 9/11 terrorist attacks changed over time and more so, were predicted by their current appraisals of the impact of the attacks. It appears that memories of past emotional responses are not always accurate, and can even be partially reconstructed based on their current of events.

Emotion Regulation Effects on Memory

An interesting issue in the study of the emotion–memory relationship is whether our emotions are influenced by our behavioural reaction to them, and whether this reaction – in the form of expression or suppression of the emotion – might in itself affects what we remember about an event.

Researchers have begun to examine whether concealing feelings influences our ability to perform common cognitive tasks, such as forming memories, and found that the emotion regulation efforts do have cognitive consequences.

In a study of Richards and Gross, participants viewed slides of injured men that produced increases in negative emotions, while information concerning each man was presented orally with his slide. The participants were assigned to either an expressive suppression group (where they were asked to refrain from showing emotion while watching the slides) or to a control group (where they were not given regulatory instructions at all).

As predicted by the researchers, suppressors showed significantly worse performance on a memory test for the orally presented information. Several related studies have reached similar results. It was demonstrated that the effects of expressive suppression on memory generalise to emotionally positive experiences and to socially relevant contexts.

One possible answer to the question "why does emotion suppression impair memory?" might lay in the self monitoring efforts invested in order to suppress emotion (thinking about the behaviour one is trying to control). A recent study found heightened self- monitoring efforts among suppressors relative to control participants.

That is, suppressors were more likely to report thinking about their behaviour and the need to control it during a conversation. Increases in self-monitoring predicted decreases in memory for what was said, that is, people who reported thinking a lot about controlling their behaviour had particularly impoverished memories. However, additional research is needed to confirm whether self-monitoring actually exerts a causal effect on memory

Emotion-induced Forgetting

Emotionally arousing stimuli can lead to retrograde amnesia for preceding events and anterograde amnesia for subsequent events. This has been demonstrated in lab studies with lists of words or pictures, in which people show impaired memory for stimuli appearing before or after arousing stimuli.

Depression and Memory

Memory recall tends to be congruent with one's current mood, with depressed people more likely to recall negative events from the past In addition, depression is often associated with poor memory in general, as outlined here.

Aging and Emotional Memory

Enhancing effects of emotional arousal on later memory recall tend to be maintained among older adults and the amygdala shows relatively less decline than many other brain regions. However, older adults also show somewhat of a shift towards favouring positive over negative information in memory, leading to a positivity effect.

■■■

Chapter 4

Putting your Memory to Work

Memory is one of the most remarkable and powerful features of human beings. Try to imagine what our everyday world would be like without memory. We would not be able to recognise people, places or things.

And without memory we would not be able to develop or even employ language. Most people would like to have better memories. And this is also true of students — especially at test time.

The Phases or Operations of Memory

We must begin by distinguishing among three operations implied by any act of remembering. These three distinct operations must have occurred in order to remember anything. The first operation of memory is acquisition.

To remember, one must first have experienced a particular object or encountered a specific piece of information. In terms of study habits, this means paying close attention to materials presented in lectures or encountered while reading your textbooks or other supplemental materials.

The second operation of memory is retention. This is the phase during which information is stored away for later use. This is the critical phase of memory. To be retained for any length of time information must be carefully organised.

For the classroom student, retention requires intense concentration and efficient study habits which assist you in organising material in a way which permits you to grasp the relationships between discrete facts.

The final operation of memory is retrieval, the phase during which one attempts to remember, or recall, some specific piece of information. As a student, you must develop study habits which enable you to acquire information in the first place, store it away for later use, and retrieve it upon demand.

Most "memory lapses" —failures to recall what the textbook or professor said —are actually retrieval problems. Retrieval problems usually result from the haphazard or disorganised storing of information. The memory simply doesn't know where to search for it.

The Three Memory Systems

Cognitive psychologists generally agree that there are three memory systems: these systems include (1) the sensory registers, (2) the short-term and (3) the long-term memory. These three memory systems are actually very interdependent rather than separate and independent systems.

We are constantly surrounded by sensory stimuli. We seldom notice many of these stimuli —the temperature in the room, the bird chirping outside the window, the car passing on the street. Memory, in the form of the sensory registers, actually comes into playas soon as we begin to focus our attention on any specific sensory stimulus. But the sensory registers hold sensory information for mere fractions of a second. Information from these sensory registers either must be transmitted immediately into the short-term memory or be lost forever.

The short-term and long-term memory systems differ from one another in terms of *(a)* their relation to our lived experience, *(b)* their storage capacity, and *(c)* the form in which information is stored. The short-term memory system deals with experiences in the very recent past. It can only hold material for about a minute or so.

And it is limited to a capacity of about seven items. Try to remember, for example, a random set of seven to ten numbers. Finally the short-term memory can hold material in a disorganised or chaotic form. The long-term memory system deals with experiences in the remote past which is viewed as gone and done with. The long-term memory, in contrast to the short-term, has an enormous capacity. It can store material for much longer periods, perhaps even for a lifetime. It holds material in a processed or organised form.

Comparison of the Short-term and Long-term Memory

Characteristic	**Short-term memory**	**Long-term memory**
lived experience	recent past	remote past
capacity	limited to seven items	virtually unlimited
storage form	may be disorganised or chaotic	must be processed or organised

A very useful analogy by which to understand these three memory systems is to think of a truck delivering items to a warehouse. The truck represents the sensory data coming towards us from the outside world. The warehouse represents our long-term memory where packages of information may be stored for long time periods. Outside the warehouse are the loading dock and the dock foreman. The dock foreman represents the sensory registers. The foreman decides which items are unloaded from the truck and placed on the loading dock. And the loading dock, of course, represents the short-term memory where packages of information are temporarily stored.

Memory Improving Techniques

One way to improve your memory is by the use of external aids, such as reference books, calendars, address books, a well marked (or 'educated') textbook, classnotes, course outlines, summaries, charts, or study guides.

Anything we learn to write down to locate at a later time is a thing we need not commit to memory. External aids are any physical devices that help us remember.

The important thing is to transfer information from the fleeting sensory registers (where it 'is being seen') or the temporary short-term memory (where it has 'just been seen') into the more permanent long-term memory.

The trick is to organise the material so it can be stored and recalled when needed. Several memory techniques can assist you in organising information for memory transference.

One of the oldest transfer techniques is repetition, especially in the form of flash or note-cards. Many students have used flashcards to learn arithmetic tables, or vocabulary cards for foreign language. You can develop a similar system for learning important definitions or lists of things. Simply put the word to be learned or the title of a list on one side of the card and the definition or the list on the other side.

Another transfer technique is known as chunking. Chunking is a technique for grouping several items of information into one piece that is as easy to remember as a single item. It is easier to remember a seven digit phone number, such as 354-2783, when it is grouped as three chunks of information, such as "three fifty four, twenty seven, and eighty three. " It is easier to remember "the three primary causes of cancer" than just "causes of cancer."

Identifying the number of items to be remembered seems to place boundaries around the material, rendering it into a "chunk" of information.

A third transfer technique is the use of mnemonics (ne-mon'-iks), which are deliberately created associations. In general terms, mnemonics are mental techniques which provide organisation in terms of which we can more easily remember information that has little rhyme or reason for us. The simplest mnemonics are the use of catchwords or catch phrases.

A catchword is a word that is made up of the first letters of several words you want to remember. You may have heard of the great advice to explain things with a "KISS," (Keep It Simple Stupid). Some catchwords become recognised as acronyms such as WAC (Women's Army Corp) etc.

A catch phrase or sentence, on the other hand, is one which the first letters of each word in the phrase correspond to the first letter of an item to be remembered. The order of the planets from the sun, for example, can be remembered by the catch phrase "Mary Visits Every Monday and Just Stays Until Noon Period" (Mercury, Venus, Earth, Mars, etc.).

Young music students are taught to remember the lines of the treble clef by means of the catch sentence "Every Good Boy Does Fine" and the spaces by the catchword " FACE." Mnemonics rely on deliberately created, even contrived, associations. Many lists of things can be so transformed into catchy mnemonics with a little effort.

Mnemonics are highly effective in memorising limited amounts of information; but alas, they do not enable us to deal with the vast amounts of wide-ranging materials we learn and need in daily life or in difficult courses. What does help us to remember large amounts of material is hierarchical organisation.

Hierarchical organisation requires active learning. It may be likened to the development of a structural framework in which the more important or general information is listed and then less important or specific information is listed below in order of decreasing generality.

A good example is the classification system utilised in biology. All living organisms are divided into broad kingdoms (e.g., plants and animals), each kingdom is divided into phyla (e.g., animals are broken down into protozoa, mollusks, anthropods, vertebrates, etc.), each phylum is divided into classes (e.g. vertebrates are divided into fish, amphibians, reptiles, mammals, etc.), and each class is further divided into orders, orders into families, families into genus, and genus into species.

The hierarchical organisation or arrangement of information is one of the most basic and strongest techniques for developing the long-term memory because it involves weaving information into a web.

And this weaving of information forces you to become an active learner, looking for your own organisational patterns.

New information can not only be inserted into the web, but becomes caught and held like a fly in a spider's web. The hierarchical organisation of information furnishes the mind with a multitude of associations or retrieval clues.

If you pull on any strand of the web, the rest of the information on that strand follows.

An example will illustrate both the nature and the value of hierarchical classification or organisation. Gave half the members of a group three minutes to memorise the following list of items:

French horn	Carnation	Birch	Trumpet	Tree
Mum	Pine	Piano	Brass	Tuba
String	Saxophone	Clarinet	Maple	Rose
Tulip	Flower	Trombone	Violin	Ash
Plant	Oak		Daisy	Reed
Harp			Instrument	

After the three minutes this group was able to write only an average of 16 words on the list. The other half of the group was given the same three minutes to memorise the same list of items, only they were organised in the following manner:

Instrument			Plant	
String	Brass	Reed	Flower	Tree
Harp	French horn	Clarinet	Mum	Pine
Piano	Trombone	Saxophone	Tulip	Oak
Violin	Trumpet		Carnation	Birch
	Tuba		Daisy	Maple
			Rose	Ash

After three minutes the members of this second group were able to write an average of 22 words on the list. And, more importantly, the members of this second group were able to recall an average of 19 words on the list a week later, whereas the first group was able to recall an average of only 7 words a week later. Apparently nothing is as productive of the effective and long-term retrieval of information as its hierarchical arrangement.

The Secret Principles for a Super Power Memory

The Greeks so worshipped memory that they made a goddess out of her — Mnemosyne. It was her name from which was derived the current word mnemonics, used to describe memory techniques such as those you are about to learn.

In Greek and Roman times, senators would learn these techniques in order to impress other politicians and the public with their phenomenal powers of learning and memory. Using these simple but sophisticated methods, the Romans were able to remember, without fault, thousands of items, including statistics relating to their empire, and became the rulers of their time.

Long before we had discovered the physiological breakdown of the functions in the left and right hemispheres of our brains, the Greeks had intuitively realised that there are two underlying principles that ensure perfect memory:

1. Imagination
2. Association

Whereas, in current times, most of us are actively discouraged from using our imaginative abilities, and consequently learn very little about the nature of mental association, the Greeks emphasised these two foundation stones of mental functioning and opened the way for us to develop the techniques even further.

Quite simply, if you want to remember anything, all you have to do is to associate (link) it with some known or fixed item.

The Rules

The rules for perfect memory laid down by the Greeks fit in exactly with the information recently discovered about the left and right brains. Without a scientific basis, the Greeks realised that in order to remember well, you have to use every aspect of your mind. In order to remember well, you must include in your associated and linked mental landscape the following:

Colour

The more colours you use, and the more vivid they are, the better. Using colour alone can improve your memory by as much as 50 percent.

Imagination

Your imagination is the powerhouse of your memory. The

more vividly you can imagine, the more easily you will remember. Sub-areas within imagination include the following:

(a) Expansion: the more gigantic and enormous you can make your mental images, the better.

(b) Contraction: if you can clearly imagine your picture as extremely tiny, you will remember it well.

(c) Absurdity: the more ridiculous, zany and absurd your mental images are, the more they will be outstanding and thus the more they will be remembered.

Rhythm

The more rhythm and variation of rhythm in your mental picture, the more that picture will weave itself into your memory.

Movement

As often as possible, try to make your mental images move. Moving objects are usually remembered better than still ones.

The Senses

Tasting

Touching

Smelling

Seeing

Hearing

The more you can involve all your senses in your memory image, the more you will remember it. For example, if you have to remember that you have to buy bananas, you stand a far better chance of not forgetting your task if you can actually imagine smelling a banana as you touch it with your hands, bite into it with your mouth and taste it, see it as it is approaching your face, and hear yourself munching it.

Sex

Sex is one of your strongest drives, and if you apply this aspect of yourself to your magnificent day-dreaming ability, your memory will improve.

Sequencing and Ordering

Imagination alone is not enough for memory. In order to function well, your mind needs order and sequence. This helps it to categorise and structure things in such a way as to make them more easily accessible, much in the same way as an ordered filing system allows easier retrieval of information than if that same information were simply dumped randomly on the floor.

Number

To make ordering and sequencing easier, it is often advisable to use numbers.

Dimension

Use your right-brain ability to see your memory images in 3-D.

Key Memory Image Words

In each memory system there is a Key Word. This word is the 'Key Memory Word' in that it is the constant peg on which the reader will hang other items he or she wishes to remember. This Key Memory Word is specifically designed to be an 'Image Word' in that it must produce a picture or image in the mind of the person using the memory system. Thus, the phrase 'Key Memory Image Word'.

As you progress through the increasingly sophisticated mnemonic systems, you will realise the importance of being sure that the pictures you build in your mind contain only the items you want to remember, and those items must be associated with or connected to Key Memory Images. The connections between your basic Memory System Images and the things you wish to remember should be as fundamental and uncomplicated as possible:

1. Crashing things together
2. Sticking things together
3. Placing things on top of each other
4. Placing things underneath each other
5. Placing things inside each other
6. Substituting things for each other
7. Placing things in new situations

By now it will be clear to you that the systems worked out by the Greeks, and for nearly 2000 years discarded as mere tricks, were in fact based on the way in which the human brain actually functions.

The ancients realised the importance of words, order, sequence and number, now known to be functions of the left side of the brain; and of imagination, colour, rhythm, dimension and daydreaming, now known to be right-brain functions.

Mnemosyne was to the Greeks the most beautiful of all the goddesses, proved by the fact that Zeus spent more time in her bed than in that of any other goddess or mortal. He slept with her for nine days and nights, and the result of that coupling was the birth of the nine Muses, the goddesses who preside over love poetry, epic poetry, hymns, dance, comedy, tragedy, music, history and astronomy. For the Greeks, then, the infusion of energy (Zeus) into memory (Mnemosyne) produced both creativity and knowledge.

They were correct. If you apply the mnemonic principles and techniques appropriately, not only will your memory improve in the various areas outlined in this book but your creativity, your overall mental functioning and assimilation of knowledge will accelerate at the same fantastic pace.

In the process you will be developing a new and dynamic synthesis between the left and right side of your brain.

The Laws of Memory

The Law of Comprehension

This is the simplest, but also the most important. According to a German writer, people poorly remember what they read because "they do too little thinking". The more deeply you grasp what you memorise, the more easily and the more in detail it will remain in your memory.

The Law of Interest

"For knowledge to be digested, it must be absorbed with relish," wrote a thinker. The interesting and "the appetising" are remembered easily as man does not have to make special efforts, as the ability to spontaneously memorise comes into play.

The Law of Previous Knowledge

The more one knows on a certain subject, the more easily one memorises everything new pertaining to it. Everyone must have noticed that when he opens a book read long ago, he reads it as if he had never read it before.

This means that when anyone read it for the first time he lacked the relevant experience and information but by this time he has accumulated them. Thus, reading forms connections between the accumulated and the new knowledge. This is the result of memorisation.

The Law of Readiness for Memorisation

The reader derives the information he sets out to derive from the text. The same goes for the duration of memorisation. When one wants to remember something for long, one will remember it in any case better than when one wants to remember something for a brief while.

The Law of Associations

This was formulated back in the 4th century B.C. by Aristotle. The concepts which arose simultaneously summon each other up from the memory bank by association.

For instance, the atmosphere of a room evokes recollections about events which took place in it (or recollection of what you read staying in it, and this is exactly what you need).

The Law of Sequences

The alphabet is easy to recite in its regular order and difficult in the reverse order. The conceptions learned in a certain sequence, when recalled, summon each other up in the same sequence.

The Law of Strong Impressions

The stronger the first impression of what is being memorised, the brighter the image. The greater the number of information channels, the more strongly the information is retained. Hence, the task is to achieve the strongest possible initial impression of the material subject.

The Law of Inhibition

Any subsequent memorisation inhibits the previous. The learned portion of information must "settle" before the next is taken up. The best way to forget newly memorised material is by trying to memorise something similar directly afterwards. This is why school children are advised not to learn physics after mathematics and literature after history and to learn poetry before going to bed.

Memorisation Advice

Before you set about reading a book, article or document, try to guess from its title what is written in it (or what you would write in the author's place). The same "forecasting" applies to the heads of chapters and the first paragraphs of the text.

Before reading (listening and glancing through) think of what information you want to derive, and what for. This will stimulate your interest and prepare you for its cognition. Where the author, citing a number of arguments, is going to draw a conclusion, make a deduction yourself first and only then continue to read.

Before reading recall all relevant information known to you. In other words, "brush up" your knowledge. Try to imitate Ancient Roman orators, who learned their speeches pacing up and down and "establishing connections" between the text and the atmosphere of their homes and then would recall the speech by taking "mental strolls". If you want to memorise a text in detail don't learn it piecemeal. Learn the whole text, and learn it in its natural sequence.

To avoid forgetting the name of a new acquaintance, strengthen the first impression left by him by repeating his name aloud ("Excuse me, have I heard you right?"), using it in the conversation and when parting. Write down this name, if only with your finger in the air. Imagine in whose honour this man may have been named, etc.

Try to evoke the strongest possible emotions connected with the information you memorise. Incidentally, this is exactly what Lenin did. The margins of the books he read bristle with categorical and profoundly emotional notes: "True!", "What nonsense!", "Ha-ha!", and "You've hit the nail on the head!"

When preparing for intensive mental efforts consider the state you are in at the moment. Sadness, irritation, uncertainty and fear are enemies of memory. Never write down things without an attempt to grasp and memorise them! To these rules you may add a host of your own, based on the laws of memory. In short, the knowledge of these laws will enable you to memorise much more than before even if you had complaints about your memory.

■■■

CHAPTER 5

Don't Be an Absent-minded

Absent-mindedness

Absent-mindedness can refer to three very different things:

1. A low level of attention ("blanking" or "zoning out");
2. Intense attention to a single object of focus (hyperfocus) that makes them oblivious to events around them; or
3. Unwarranted distraction of attention from the object of focus by irrelevant thoughts or environmental events.

Consequences

Lapses of attention are clearly a part of everyone's life. Some are merely inconvenient, such as missing a familiar turn-off on the highway, and some are extremely serious, such as failures of attention that cause accidents, injury, or loss of life.

Beyond the obvious costs of accidents arising from lapses in attention there is lost time, efficiency, personal productivity, and quality of life in the lapse and recapture of awareness and attention to everyday tasks. Individuals for whom intervals between lapses are very short are typically viewed as impaired . Given the prevalence of attentional failures in everyday life and the ubiquitous and sometimes disastrous consequences of such failures, it is rather surprising that relatively little work has been done to directly measure individual differences in everyday errors arising from propensities for failures of attention.

Memory Aspects

Absent-mindedness is related to memory failures. For example, Schachter treats absent-mindedness as one of the seven sins of memory created by Daniel Schacter. It is specifically under the subcategory, sin of omission.

Absent-mindedness is simply a failure in attention, involving an overlap between both attention and memory in both the encoding and retrieval stage of memory.

Absent-minded memory failures occur when one is distracted with issues or concerns, and he/she is unable to focus on things needed to remember. For example, Schacter exemplified the conditions of misplacing one's keys or glasses.

It is clear, however, even from this brief description, that the primary problem in absent-mindedness is one of attention. Recent research has reported that attention lapses may be direct causes of both memory failures as well as action slips.

Quick Memory Tips

Here are some solutions you can use to improve your memory right now. There are lots of other steps you can take to improve your memory even more. Here are steps you can take immediately.

To remember things better:

1. Pay close attention,
2. Use all of your senses,
3. Recite the material,
4. Have confidence in your memory.

Increase your Attention/Concentration

Your "attention" is how tightly you focus on new information. We can tell you right now that if you are not focusing intently – if your mind is wandering or you are "out of it" – you are not going to remember well.

What you want to do is increase your brain's power of concentration, plus you want to be able to crank this up whenever you need to.

Below are some quick fixes for increasing your concentration right now.

- **Take breaths from your belly:** Many people are shallow breathers and don't know it. Take several deep, slow breaths from your belly. Stomach breathing activates the brains Theta waves, which research shows improves memory. Deep breathing also increases the oxygen flow to your brain cells, which helps "wake them up".
- **Chew a piece of gum:** According to research, the act of chewing gum increases the flow of blood to your brain.

  Researchers have shown that people chewing gum are able to concentrate more intently and remember new information better. Chew the sugar-free type to avoid a blood sugar spike.

- **Do arm circles:** Go where no one can see you (for example, the bathroom) and do 10 sets of arm circles. To do an arm circle, simply extend your arm straight out, then swing your arm all the way around behind you and back to the front, keeping your elbow locked. Do 10 on each side.

  This move only takes about 30 seconds but will increase your heart rate and the flow of blood to your brain.

- **Play a brain game:** Puzzles and brain teasers force your mind to get in concentration mode. My favourite is Sudoku (a number puzzle).

- **Eat a brain snack or meal:** A meal heavy on carbs and sugar will kill your concentration because of the way it spikes (and then crashes) your blood sugar. Similarly, skipping meals tends to make you light-headed.

  Instead, eat a small, balanced meal. Include foods that help the brain operate well, such as fish, vegetables, and whole grains.

- **Drink a litre of water:** Don't drink sodas. Don't drink coffee. Don't eat a candy bar. These will not improve your concentration, they will just cause you to crash. Instead – get a litre bottle of water, and drink the entire thing straight down.

  Many people are dehydrated all the time and don't realise it. Your brain is very sensitive to this. Drink that bottle of water, and we guarantee you'll be more alert.

- **Use "time boxes":** When you need to study new information, sit down in a quiet spot and set a timer. Give yourself only "X" amount of time to read review the material (for example, a half an hour for a magazine article).

  Break it down further – say 10 minutes to read an article, then 20 minutes to review and recite the information. Having a timer going and a predefined "time box" forces you to focus, because you know that your time is limited!

Use All of Your Senses

Are you concentrating now? Good, here are quick ways to actually remember the information better. Realise that different parts of your brain remember different sense impressions.

For example, images are stored in one area, sounds in another, and tactile (touch) sensations in another. What you want to do is plug new information into your brain using as many different senses as possible.

The idea is that you can build multiple memory pathways to the information. For example, if you fail to remember the material through sight, then your audio pathway may allow you to access it.

The more sensory pathways you engage, the more likely you will later be able to jog your memory and recall the information.

Do all of these steps (or as many as possible) with any new material you want to remember:

1. **See it!** This is the easy one most of the time. When you are reading, you are seeing the information. For non-

written material or physical items, use your new ability to concentrate to really see the item.

Look carefully and slowly at the shape, colour, texture of the object, the material it's made of.

2. **Say it!** Read new material out loud. Find a secluded place, perhaps at home, so you don't distract others. Reading out loud causes memory pathways to form not only through the visual sense (you see the words on the paper), but also through hearing the words. You now have two ways to recall the information.
3. **Write it!** Write down critical concepts. This is also known as note-taking. The act of writing is a physical action that stimulates specific pathways in the brain.
4. **Do it!** If it's a procedure you need to remember, do it. Do it several times. The act of "doing" is a separate mental pathway that you create. Just reading about something (or just hearing someone else explain how to do it) is not good enough.
5. **Draw it!** Can the information be associated with one or more images? Draw them, even if you are not an artist. Just the act of sketching on paper, even silly images, will engage your visual and creative memory - giving you yet another path for remembering the material.
6. **Imagine it!** Imagine (visualise) the material you want to remember. Studying chemistry or atomic theory? Try to see in your mind's eye the electrons spinning around the atomic nuclei, try to visualise the molecules you are studying about. Learning history?

   Try to imagine what the battle must have been like, the location, the combatants, what they were wearing, and their weapons. Make it real to you. Bring it out of the abstract.

7. **Research it!** Pull even more brain pathways into the situation. Go on the Internet and research examples. Find more detail than your book or your instructor or that article your read about explained. The more interconnections you can make in your brain by linking information together, the better you will remember.

8. **Emotionalise it!** Find some way to become "connected" with the material. Look for ways to relate emotionally.

   Anything emotional will be a lot easier to remember. It can make you sad or happy or excited or intrigued. It doesn't matter, but you must find some way to care about the material.

9. **Convert it!** Trying to memorise dry facts, like dates, numbers, and formulas? Find patterns in the information and convert these to something meaningful. For example, try to create rhymes, try to match up the details with facts you already know, patterns can even be found in the shapes of numbers and formulas if you study them closely.

10. **Question it!** Don't be a passive and take everything dished out to you. Question the validity of new material. Ask yourself how this or that fact is known, what is the evidence? Is it believable?

    What does it imply, and how does it relate to what you already know? By questioning material you make it your own and you make it much more memorable.

    When reading a chapter in a book, scan the headings and turn each backwards into a question. Then when you read the chapter, look for the answers.

Recite to Remember

Recite, recite, and recite. To recite means repeating within a few minutes and hours what you have just learned. Studies show that most forgetting occurs within just a few minutes. If you recite the information, instead of forgetting it you will be more likely save it in long-term memory.

Don't just passively reread the material, either. Say it out loud from memory, or write it down from memory.

Here are some tools that work well for reciting:

1. **Make flash cards.** As you study, write key facts on index cards. On the front, write the name of the concept, then on the back, write the details.

   During and after each study session, flip through your stacks of cards and test your knowledge.

2. **Repeat in your head.** When listening to a lecture, the radio, or other source of audible information, repeat the information mentally as you hear it.

   After each sentence spoken by the instructor, for example, say the sentence back to yourself in your head. This doubles the number of times you hear new information, plus it makes you an active participant.

3. **Rephrase and reuse.** Shortly after learning anything new, reuse it in your own way using your own words. For example, when you meet someone new, use their name in the conversation one or two times to help you remember it.

4. **Quiz yourself.** Every time you learn something new, give yourself a quick quiz within a few minutes. Every few minutes, pause and force you to say back what you've just studied or heard.

If you can't remember much, that means you need to go back and read or study it more closely. You are wasting your time if you are not actually learning the information as you go along.

5. **Teach it.** If you can teach it so that someone else understands, that means you know it. If possible, teach someone else the details of what you've learned, soon after you learn it.

   In a school situation, this means joining a study group and volunteering often to be the "explainer". Or, become a tutor.

Be Confident

If you're not careful, you can be your own worst enemy when it comes to remembering things. The power of **positive thinking** is real - and so is the power of *negative* thinking. If you continually tell yourself you have a bad memory, eventually you will start to believe it!

The next time you catch yourself thinking negatively about your memory, just stop. Instead, actively shift your internal dialogue in a more positive direction. Tell yourself, "I *can* remember this material. I can do this!"

How to Stop Being Absent-minded

If you're absent-minded, the cat may miss his breakfast before you go to work, the kids may wait by the curb for their ride and the boss may show you the door...and not kindly. The good news is – you can change your forgetfulness into a cutting-edge memory...with a little help.

Instructions

Step 1

Get organised. Absent-minded folks really hate recording dates on their calendar or carrying a digital recorder around but it works. Just don't forget to put the recorder or daybook in your briefcase.

Step 2

Teach yourself to identify an appointment or chore with a mental trigger. This is an old trick that really jogs the memory. For example, if you have to pick up milk on the way home, imagine yourself getting into your car that looks like a big momma cow and driving to the grocery.

Step 3

Put things in their place or don't put them down. The next time you think to yourself, "Hmmm...I'll just put my glasses behind the TV for a minute," think again – that little habit-breaker ensures you'll be hunting for your spectacles within the hour. Get-off your lazy duff and carry them to their case by the bed. Then you can return to the sofa and snooze.

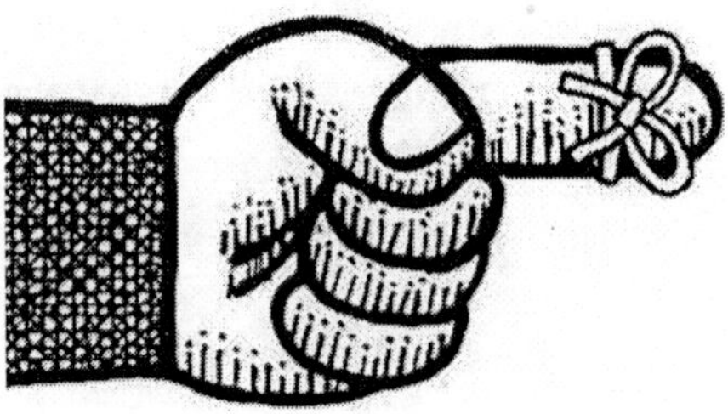

Step 4

Prioritise the things in your life and get rid of the cluttering details that only distract you. Yes, you have to remember your hair cut appointment; no, you don't have to run by the movie rental store to choose a video for the kids or exchange Fido's collar for a hot pink one. If too many fluffy details are bogging you down - cut them out.

Step 5

Pick up a book of crossword puzzles or logic games. Exercising your mind keeps you mentally healthy and happy. Do it for fun and when it becomes tiresome, set it aside.

Step 6

Rate your appointments in the order of importance. In your daybook, give the most important items three stars and the least important ones only one star.

When you're pressed for time, opt to do the most important and don't berate yourself that you couldn't do everything.

Improve your Memory

If our brains were computers, we'd simply add a chip to upgrade our memory. However, the human brain is more complex than even the most advanced machine, so improving human memory requires slightly more effort.

Just like muscular strength, your ability to remember increases when you exercise your memory and nurture it with a good diet and other healthy habits. There are a number of steps you can take to improve your memory and retrieval capacity. However, it's helpful to understand how we remember.

Stages of Memory Foundation and Maintenance

There are three stages that the brain goes through in forming and retaining memories.

Acquisition

New information enters your brain along pathways between neurons in the appropriate area of the brain. The key to encoding information into your memory is concentration; unless you focus on information intently, it goes "in one ear and out the other." This is why teachers are always nagging students to pay attention!

Consolidation

If you've concentrated well enough to encode new information in your brain, the hippocampus sends a signal to store the information as long-term memory. This happens more easily if it's related to something you already know, or if it stimulates an emotional response.

Retrieval

When you need to recall information, your brain has to activate the same pattern of nerve cells it used to store it. The more frequently you need the information, the easier it is to retrieve it along healthy nerve cell connections.

Why do Most of us have a Bad Memory

Most of us have a really good memory, but we just don't have practice in using it efficiently.

If the above is true, then why is it so hard for me to remember things?

As stated before, our memory works by association. If there is no obvious association between things, it's very difficult to remember them. For example, suppose you needed to remember that your plane takes off at 2 P.M.

There is nothing about the plane that would suggest the number 2 more than it would any other number (at least at first glance). Therefore, 2 is easily forgotten. Likewise, how does your best friend relate to his phone number, an arbitrary string of digits? Or how does a new word, like "hypothalamus," relate to what it represents?

Tips for Memory Improvements

Do you feel that you have a poor memory? You may just have some less-than-effective habits when it comes to taking in and processing information. Barring disease, disorder, or injury, you can improve your ability to learn and retain information.

Brain Exercises

Memory, like muscular strength, is a "use it or lose it" proposition. The more you work out your brain, the better you'll be able to process and remember information.

Novelty and sensory stimulation are the foundation of brain exercise. If you break your routine in a challenging way, you're using brain pathways you weren't using before. This can involve something as simple as brushing your teeth with your non-dominant hand, which activates little-used connections on the non-dominant side of your brain.

Or try a "neurobic" exercise – an aerobic exercise for your brain that forces you to use your faculties in unusual ways, like showering and getting dressed with your eyes closed.

Take a course in a subject you don't know much about, learn a new game of strategy, or cook up some recipes in an unfamiliar cuisine. That's the most effective way to keep your synapses firing.

General Guidelines to Improve Memory

In addition to exercising your brain, there are some basic things you can do to improve your ability to retain and retrieve memories:

1. **Pay attention:** You can't remember something if you never learned it, and you can't learn something — that is, encode it into your brain — if you don't pay enough attention to it. It takes about eight seconds of intent focus to process a piece of information through your hippocampus and into the appropriate memory centre.

   So, no multitasking when you need to concentrate! If you distract easily, try to receive information in a quiet place where you won't be interrupted.

2. **Tailor information acquisition to your learning style:** Most people are visual learners; they learn best by reading or otherwise seeing what it is they have to know. But some are auditory learners who learn better by listening.

   They might benefit by recording information they need and listening to it until they remember it.

3. **Involve as many senses as possible:** Even if you're a visual learner, read out loud what you want to remember. If you can recite it rhythmically, even better. Try to relate information to colours, textures, smells and tastes. The physical act of rewriting information can help imprint it onto your brain.

4. **Relate information to what you already know:** Connect new data to information you already remember, whether it's new material that builds on previous knowledge, or something as simple as an address of someone who lives on a street where you already know someone.

5. **Organise information:** Write things down in address books and datebooks and on calendars; take notes on

more complex material and reorganise the notes into categories later. Use both words and pictures in learning information.

6. **Understand and be able to interpret complex material:** For more complex material, focus on understanding basic ideas rather than memorising isolated details. Be able to explain it to someone else in your own words.
7. **Rehearse information frequently and "over-learn":** Review what you've learned the same day you learn it, and at intervals thereafter.

   What researchers call "spaced rehearsal" is more effective than "cramming." If you're able to "over-learn" information so that recalling it becomes second nature, so much the better.
8. **Be motivated and keep a positive attitude:** Tell yourself that you *want* to learn what you need to remember, and that you *can* learn and remember it.

   Telling yourself you have a bad memory actually hampers the ability of your brain to remember, while positive mental feedback sets up an expectation of success.

Mnemonic Devices to Improve Memory

Mnemonics (the initial "m" is silent) are clues of any kind that help us remember something, usually by causing us to associate the information we want to remember with a visual image, a sentence, or a word.

Common types of mnemonic devices include:

1. **Visual images** - A microphone to remember the name "Mike," a rose for "Rosie." Use positive, pleasant images, because the brain often blocks out unpleasant ones, and

make them vivid, colourful, and three-dimensional — they'll be easier to remember.

2. **Sentences** in which the first letter of each word is part of or represents the initial of what you want to remember.

   Millions of musicians, for example, first memorised the lines of the treble staff with the sentence "Every good boy does fine" (or "deserves favour"), representing the notes E, G, B, D, and F. Medical students often learn groups of nerves, bones, and other anatomical features using nonsense sentences.

3. **Acronyms**, which are initials that creates pronounceable words. The spaces between the lines on the treble staff, for example, are F, A, C, and E: FACE.

4. **Rhymes and alliteration**: Remember learning "30 days hath September, April, June, and November"? A hefty guy named Robert can be remembered as "Big Bob" and a smiley co-worker as "Perky Pat" (though it might be best to keep such names to you).

5. **Jokes** or even off-colour associations using facts, figures, and names you need to recall, because funny or peculiar things are easier to remember than mundane images.

6. **"Chunking" information**; that is, arranging a long list in smaller units or categories that are easier to remember.

   If you can reel off your Social Security number without looking at it, that's probably because it's arranged in groups of 3, 2, and 4 digits, not a string of 9.

7. **"Method of loci"**: This is an ancient and effective way of remembering a lot of material, such as a speech. You associate each part of what you have to remember with a

landmark in a route you know well, such as your commute to work.

Healthy Habits to Improve Memory

Treating your body well can enhance your ability to process and recall information.

Healthy Habits that Improve Memory include:

Regular Exercise

- Increases oxygen to your brain.
- Reduces the risk for disorders that lead to memory loss, such as diabetes and cardiovascular disease.
- May enhance the effects of helpful brain chemicals and protect brain cells.

Managing Stress

- Cortisol, the stress hormone, can damage the hippocampus if the stress is unrelieved.
- Stress makes it difficult to concentrate.

Good Sleep Habits

- Sleep is necessary for memory consolidation.
- Sleep disorders like insomnia and sleep apnea leave you tired and unable to concentrate during the day.

Not Smoking

- Smoking heightens the risk of vascular disorders that can cause stroke and constrict arteries that deliver oxygen to the brain.

Nutrition and Memory Improvement

You probably know already that a diet based on fruits, vegetables, whole grains, and "healthy" fats will provide lots of health benefits, but such a diet can also improve memory. Research indicates that certain nutrients nurture and stimulate brain function.

B vitamins, especially B6, B12, and folic acid, protects neurons by breaking down homocysteine, an amino acid that is toxic to nerve cells. They're also involved in making red blood cells, which carry oxygen. (Best sources: spinach and other dark leafy greens, broccoli, asparagus, strawberries, melons, black beans and other legumes, citrus fruits, soybeans.)

Antioxidants like vitamins C and E, and beta carotene, fight free radicals, which are atoms formed when oxygen interacts with certain molecules.

Free radicals are highly reactive and can damage cells, but anti-oxidants can interact with them safely and neutralise them. Anti-oxidants also improve the flow of oxygen through the body and brain. (Best sources: blueberries and other berries, sweet potatoes, red tomatoes, spinach, broccoli, green tea, nuts and seeds, citrus fruits, liver.)

Omega-3 fatty acids are concentrated in the brain and are associated with cognitive function. They count as "healthy" fats, as opposed to saturated fats and trans fats, protecting against inflammation and high cholesterol. (Best sources: cold-water fish such as salmon, herring, tuna, halibut, and mackerel; walnuts and walnut oil; flaxseed and flaxseed oil)

Because older adults are more prone to B12 and folic acid deficiencies, a supplement may be a good idea for seniors. An omega-3 supplement (at any age) if you don't like eating fish. But nutrients work best when they're consumed in foods, so try your best to eat a broad spectrum of colourful plant foods and choose fats that will help clear, not clog, your arteries. Your brain will thank you!

Developing your Ability to Remember

Are you often unable to remember an important fact or figure? Do you forget people's names at the worst moments? Are you ever asked a question, and you should know the answer, but you struggle to form an intelligent reply?

These are common instances where a good memory is important.

Memory is more than recalling information for exams or trivia games. It's an important work skill that you can develop and improve.

Whether it's remembering key statistics during a negotiation, or quoting a precedent-setting action when making a decision, or impressing clients with your knowledge of their product lines - your ability to remember is a major advantage.

People with good memories are often seen as knowledgeable, smart, competent, and dependable. And there are many techniques you can use to develop your own ability to remember information - and then recall it when and where you need it.

Take Care of your Health

The basis for a good memory is a healthy mind and body. You can't expect your brain to function at its best if you don't take care of the body that feeds it. Here are some key issues that you need to address:

- **Eat well** - Make sure key vitamins are in your diet, including folic acid, vitamin B12, and anti-oxidants. These improve the sharpness of the mind. If necessary, take vitamin supplements.
- **Drink plenty of water** - Most of us are dehydrated and don't even know it. When you don't drink enough water, your body and mind become weak and tired. Water makes red blood cells more active and gives you more energy.
- **Get enough sleep** - During sleep, your brain recharges itself. Studies have shown that your brain needs sleep to change new memories into long-term memories.
- **Manage stress effectively** - Ongoing stress has many harmful health effects. Learn to limit and control the stress in your life.

  Use physical relaxation techniques, thought awareness and rational positive thinking, and imagery to reduce your levels of stress.
- **Don't smoke** - Limit caffeine and alcohol use (excessive alcohol can seriously affect your short-term memory). Get enough exercise.

These basic health tips allow you to maximise your brain's abilities.

Mind Mapping

Mind maps (also called concept maps or memory maps) are an effective way to link ideas and concepts in your brain, and then "see" the connections firsthand.

Mind mapping is a note-taking technique that records information in a way that shows you how various pieces of information fit together.

There's a lot of truth in the saying "A picture speaks a thousand words", and mind maps create an easily-remembered "picture" of the information you're trying to remember.

This technique is very useful to summarise and combine information from a variety of sources. It also allows you to think about complex problems in an organised manner, and then present your findings in a way that shows the details as well as the big picture.

The mind map itself is a useful end product. However, the process of creating the map is just as helpful for your memory.

Fitting all the pieces together, and looking for the connections, forces you to really understand what you're studying - and it keeps you from trying to simply memorise.

Challenge your Brain

As with other parts of your body, your mind needs exercise. You can exercise your brain by using it in different ways, on a regular basis. Try the following:

- **Learn a new skill or start a hobby** - Find activities that build skills you don't normally use in your daily life. For example, if you work with numbers all day, develop your creative side with art classes or photography.

- **Use visualisation on a regular basis** - Since much of memory involves associating and recalling images, it's important to build this skill. Get plenty of practice with this!
- **Keep active socially** - When you communicate and interact with people, you have to be alert. This helps keep your brain strong and alive.
- **Focus on the important things** - You can't possibly remember everything, so make sure you give your brain important things to do - and don't overload it with "waste." The "garbage in, garbage out" philosophy works well here.

Tip

While it's important to develop a good memory, remembering unnecessary things (such as tasks you need to do, or things you need to buy) is hard work.

What's more, because these consume short-term memory, they can diminish your ability to concentrate on other things. They can also leave you stressed, as you struggle to remember all of the things you have to do.

Write these things down on your to-do list! This way, you don't have to remember everything. And if your memory fails, you know where to look for the information you need.

- Keep your brain active with memory games and puzzles - Try Sudoku, Chess, Scrabble, and Word Twist as well as trivia games, pair matching, and puzzles. These are popular ways to practice memorisation while having fun.

Key Points

Your memory is a valuable asset that you should protect and develop. Even if you no longer have to memorise information for exams, the ability to remember quickly and accurately is always important.

Whether it's remembering the name of someone you met at a conference last month, or recalling the sales figure from last quarter, you must rely on your memory. Learn and practice the above techniques to keep your mind healthy.

You have only one brain - so treat it well, give it lots of exercise, and don't take it for granted. You never know when you'll need its skills to be at their best!

■■■

CHAPTER 6

Memory Improvement Techniques

This chapter teaches you useful techniques that help you improve your memory.

These tools help you remember people's names more effectively, improve your recall of information in exams, increase the speed with which you can learn vocabulary, and help you in situations where you need to remember detailed, structured information.

This chapter is split into three parts: first of all, the introduction explains the principles behind the use of memory techniques (also called "mnemonics").

We then discuss a range of individual tools that you can use to remember information. Finally, we discuss how to use the skills in practice to remember people's names, foreign language words, and information for exams.

An Introduction to Memory Techniques

The tools in this chapter help you to improve your memory.

They help you both to remember facts accurately and to remember the structure of information.

The tools are split into two parts. Firstly, you'll learn the memory techniques themselves. Secondly, we'll look at how you can use them in practice to remember peoples names, languages, exam information, and so on.

As with other mind tools, the more practice you give yourself with these techniques, the more effectively you will use them. This section contains many of the memory techniques used by stage memory performers.

With enough practice and effort, you may be able to have a memory as good. Even if you do not have the time needed to develop this quality of memory, many of the techniques here are useful in everyday life.

Mnemonics

'Mnemonic' is another word for memory tool. Mnemonics are techniques for remembering information that is otherwise quite difficult to recall: A very simple example is the '30 days hath September' rhyme for remembering the number of days in each calendar month.

The idea behind using mnemonics is to encode difficult-to-remember information in a way that is much easier to remember.

Our brains evolved to code and interpret complex stimuli such as images, colours, structures, sounds, smells, tastes, touch, positions, emotions and language. We use these to make sophisticated models of the world we live in. Our memories store all of these very effectively.

Unfortunately, a lot of information we have to remember in modern life is presented differently – as words printed on a page.

While writing is a rich and sophisticated medium for conveying complex arguments, our brains do not easily encode written information, making it difficult to remember.

Mind Tools shows you how to use all the memory resources available to you to remember information in a highly efficient way.

Using your Whole Mind to Remember

The key idea is that by coding information using vivid mental images, you can reliably code both information and the structure of information. And because the images are vivid, they are easy to recall when you need them.

The techniques explained later on show you how to code information vividly, using stories, strong mental images, familiar journeys, and so on.

You can do the following things to make your mnemonics more memorable:

- Use positive, pleasant images. Your brain often blocks out unpleasant ones.
- Use vivid, colourful, sense-laden images - these are easier to remember than drab ones.
- Use all your senses to code information or dress up an image. Remember that your mnemonic can contain sounds, smells, tastes, touch, movements and feelings as well as pictures.

- Give your image three dimensions, movement and space to make it more vivid. You can use movement either to maintain the flow of association, or to help you to remember actions.
- Exaggerate the size of important parts of the image.
- Use humour! Funny or peculiar things are easier to remember than normal ones.
- Similarly, rude rhymes are very difficult to forget!
- Symbols (red traffic lights, pointing fingers, road signs, etc.) can code quite complex messages quickly and effectively.

Designing Mnemonics: Imagination, Association and Location

The three fundamental principles underlying the use of mnemonics are imagination, association and location. Working together, you can use these principles to generate powerful mnemonic systems.

Imagination: is what you use to create and strengthen the associations needed to create effective mnemonics. Your imagination is what you use to create mnemonics that are potent for you. The more strongly you imagine and visualise a situation, the more effectively it will stick in your mind for later recall. The imagery you use in your mnemonics can be as violent, vivid, or sensual as you like, as long as it helps you to remember.

Association: this is the method by which you link a thing to be remembered to a way of remembering it. You can create associations by:

- Placing things on top of each other
- Crashing things together
- Merging images together
- Wrapping them around each other
- Rotating them around each other or having them dancing together
- Linking them using the same colour, smell, shape, or feeling

As an example, you might link the number 1 with a goldfish by visualising a 1-shaped spear being used to spear it.

Location: gives you two things: a coherent context into which you can place information so that it hangs together, and a way of separating one mnemonic from another. By setting one mnemonic in a particular town, we can separate it from a similar mnemonic set in a city.

For example, by setting one in Wimbledon and another similar mnemonic with images of Manhattan, we can separate them with no danger of confusion. You can build the flavours and atmosphere of these places into your mnemonics to strengthen the feeling of location.

The Link and Story Methods: Remembering a Simple List

The Link Method is one of the easiest mnemonic techniques available. You use it by making simple associations between items in a list, linking them with a vivid image containing the items.

Taking the first image, create a connection between it and

the next item (perhaps in your mind smashing them together, putting one on top of the other, or suchlike.) Then move on through the list linking each item with the next.

The Story Method is very similar, linking items together with a memorable story featuring them. The flow of the story and the strength of the images give you the cues for retrieval.

How to Use the Tools?

It is quite possible to remember lists of words using association only. However, it is often best to fit the associations into a story: Otherwise by forgetting just one association you can lose the whole of the rest of the list.

Given the fluid structure of this mnemonic it is important that the images stored in your mind are as vivid as possible. Where a word you want to remember does not trigger strong images, use a similar word that will remind you of that word.

Example:

In United Kingdom, you may want to remember this list of counties in the South of England: Avon, Dorset, Somerset, Cornwall, Wiltshire, Devon, Gloucestershire, Hampshire, and Surrey. You could do this with two approaches, the Link Method and the Story Method:

Remembering with the Link Method

This would rely on a series of images coding information:

- An AVON (Avon) lady knocking on a heavy oak DOOR (Dorset)
- The DOOR opening to show a beautiful SUMMER landscape with a SETting sun (Somerset)

- The setting sun shines down onto a field of CORN (Cornwall)
- The CORN is so dry it is beginning to WILT (Wiltshire)
- The WILTING stalks slowly droop onto the tail of the sleeping Devil (Devon).
- On the DEVIL'S horn a woman has impaled a GLOSSY (Gloucestershire) HAM (Hampshire) when she hit him over the head with it
- Now the DEVIL feels SORRY (Surrey) he bothered her.

Note that there need not be any reason or underlying plot to the sequence of images: only images and the links between images are important.

Remembering with the Story Method

Alternatively you could code this information by imaging the following story vividly:

An AVON lady is walking up a path towards a strange house. She is hot and sweating slightly in the heat of high SUMMER (Somerset).

Beside the path someone has planted giant CORN in a WALL (Cornwall), but it's beginning to WILT (Wiltshire) in the heat. She knocks on the DOOR (Dorset), which is opened by the DEVIL (Devon).

In the background she can see a kitchen in which a servant is smearing honey on a HAM (Hampshire), making it GLOSSY (Gloucestershire) and gleam in bright sunlight streaming in through a window. Panicked by seeing the Devil, the Avon lady screams 'SORRY' (Surrey), and dashes back down the path.

Key Points

The Link Method is probably the most basic memory technique, and is very easy to understand and use. It works by coding information to be remembered into images and then linking these images together.

The story technique is very similar. It links these images together into a story. This helps to keep events in a logical order and can improve your ability to remember information if you forget the sequence of images.

Both techniques are very simple to learn. Unfortunately they are both slightly unreliable as it is easy to confuse the order of images or forget images from a sequence.

The Number/Rhyme Mnemonic: Remembering Simple Ordered Lists

A Popular Peg System

The Number/Rhyme technique is a very simple way of remembering lists in order.

It is an example of a peg system using – a system where information is 'pegged' to a known sequence (here the numbers one to ten) to create pegwords.

By doing this you ensure that you do not forget any facts, as gaps in information are immediately obvious. It also makes remembering images easier as you always know part of the mnemonic images.

At a simple level you can use it to remember things such as a list of Indian Kings or American Presidents in their precise order. At a more advanced level it can be used, for example, to code lists of experiments to be recalled in a science exam.

How to Use the Tool:

The technique works by helping you to build up pictures in your mind, in which you represent numbers by things that rhyme with the number. You can then link these pictures to images of the things to be remembered.

The usual rhyming scheme is:

1. Bun
2. Shoe
3. Tree
4. Paw
5. Hive
6. Bricks
7. Heaven
8. Gate
9. Line
10. Hen

If you find that these images do not attract you or stick in your mind, then change them for something more meaningful.

Link these images to ones representing the things to be remembered. Often, the sillier the compound image, the more effectively you will remember it.

Example:

For example, you could remember a list of ten Greek philosophers as:

1. Parmenides – a BUN topped with grated yellow parmesan cheese.

2. Heraclitus – a SHOE worn by heracles (Greek Hercules) glowing with a bright light.
3. Empedocles – a TREE from which the M-shaped McDonald's arches hang hooking up a bicycle pedal.
4. Democritus – a PAW print on the voting form of a democratic election.
5. Protagoras – a bee HIVE being hit by an atomic proton.
6. Socrates – BRICKS falling onto a sock (with a foot inside!) from a crate.
7. Plato – a plate with angel's wings flapping around a white cloud.
8. Aristotle – a GATE being jumped by a bewigged French aristocrat carrying a bottle.
9. Zeno – a LINE of zen Buddhists meditating.
10. Epicurus – a flying HEN carrying an epidemic's cure.

Try either visualising these images as suggested, or if you do not like them, come up with images of your own. Once you have done this, try writing down the names of the philosophers on a piece of paper.

You should be able to do this by thinking of the number, then the part of the image associated with the number, and then the whole image. Finally, you can decode the image to give you the name of the philosopher.

If the mnemonic has worked, you should not only recall the names of all the philosophers in the correct order, but should also be able to spot where you have left them out of the sequence. Try it – it's easier than it sounds.

You can use a peg system like this as a basis for knowledge

in an entire area. The example above could form the basis for knowledge of ancient philosophy. You could now associate images representing the projects, systems and theories of each philosopher with the images coding the philosophers' names.

Key Points

The Number/Rhyme technique is a very effective method of remembering lists. It works by 'pegging' the things to be remembered to images rhyming with the numbers 0-9. By driving the associations with numbers you have a good starting point in reconstructing the images, you are aware if information is missing, and you can pick up and continue the sequence from anywhere within the list.

The Number/Shape Mnemonic: Remembering Simple Ordered Lists

The Number/Shape system is very similar to the Number/Rhyme system. It is a very simple and effective way of remembering a list in a specific order. It is another example of a peg system based on pegword images.

How to Use the Tool:

The technique works by helping you to build up pictures in your mind, in which the numbers are represented by images shaped like the number. You can then associate these with the things you want to remember using striking images.

One image scheme is shown below:

1. Candle, spear, stick
2. Swan (beak, curved neck, body)
3. Bifocal glasses, or part of a "love heart"

4. Sail of a yacht
5. A meat hook, a sea-horse facing right
6. A golf club
7. A cliff edge
8. An egg timer
9. A balloon with a string attached, flying freely
10. A hole

If you find that these images do not attract you or stick in your mind, then change them for something more meaningful to you.

As with the Number/Rhyme scheme, link these images to ones representing the things to be remembered.

In some cases these images may be more vivid than those in the number/rhyme scheme, and in other cases you may find the number/rhyme scheme more memorable. There is no reason why you cannot mix the most vivid images of each scheme together into your own compound scheme.

Example:

We can use a list of modern thinkers to illustrate the number/shape system:

1. Spinoza - a large CANDLE wrapped around with someone's spine
2. Locke - a SWAN trying to pick a lock with its wing
3. Hume - a human child with BIFOCAL glasses
4. Berkeley - a SAIL on top of a large hooked and spiked burr in the lee of a cliff
5. Kant - a can of spam hanging from a meat HOOK

6. Rousseau - a kangaroo sewing with a GOLF CLUB
7. Hegel - a crooked trader about to be pushed over a CLIFF, haggling to try to avoid being hurt
8. Kierkegaard - a large EGG TIMER containing captain Kirk and a guard from the starship enterprise, as time runs out
9. Darwin - a BALLOON floating upwards, being blown far by the wind
10. Wittgenstein - a HOLE with a witty general in it holding a stein of beer.

Key Points

The Number/Shape technique is a very effective method of remembering lists. It works by linking things to be remembered with the images representing the numbers 0-9. By using it in conjunction with the Number/Rhyme system, you can build potent images that can make very effective mnemonics.

The Alphabet Technique: Remembering Simple Ordered Lists

A Popular Pegword System

The Alphabet system is a peg memory technique similar to, but more sophisticated than, the Number/Rhyme system. It is a good method for remembering longer lists of items in a specific order, in such a way that you can tell if items are missing.

It works by associating images representing letters of the alphabet with images you create for the things to be remembered.

How to Use the Tool:

When you are creating images for the letters of the alphabet, create images phonetically, so that the sound of the first syllable of the word is the name of the letter. For example, you might represent the letter 'k' with the word 'cake'.

Tony Buzan, in his book Use Your Perfect Memory, suggests using a system for creating vivid images that you can reconstruct if you forget them. He suggests taking the phonetic letter sound as the first consonant, and then, for the rest of the consonants in the word, using the first letters in alphabetical order that make a memorable word.

For example for the letter 'S' (root 'Es') we would first see if any strong images presented themselves when we tried to create a word starting with 'EsA', 'EsB', 'EsC', 'EsD', 'EsE', etc.).

This approach has the advantage of producing an image that you can reconstruct if you forget it. You might, however, judge that this is an unnecessary complication of a relatively simple system. In any case it is best to select the strongest image that comes to mind and stick with it.

One image scheme is shown below:

A	-	Ace of spades
B	-	Bee
C	-	Sea
D	-	Diesel engine
E	-	Eel
F	-	Effluent
G	-	Jeans
H	-	H-Bomb, itch

I	-	Eye
J	-	Jade
K	-	Cake
L	-	Elephant
M	-	Empty
N	-	Entrance
O	-	Oboe
P	-	Pea
Q	-	Queue
R	-	Ark
S	-	Eskimo
T	-	Teapot
U	-	Unicycle
V	-	Vehicle
W	-	WC
X	-	X-Ray
Y	-	Wire
Z	-	Zulu

If you find that these images do not attract you or stick in your mind, then change them for something more meaningful to you.

Once you have firmly visualised these images and have linked them to their root letters, you can associate them with information to be remembered.

Example:

Continuing our mnemonic example of the names of philosophers, we will use the example of remembering a list of modern thinkers:

A - Ace - Freud - a crisp ACE being pulled out of a frying pan (fried)

B - Bee - Chomsky - a BEE stinging a chimp and flying off into the SKY

C - Sea - Genette - a gererator being lifted in a NET out of the SEA

D - Diesel - Derrida - a daring rider surfing on top of a DIESEL train

E - Eagle - Foucault - Bruce Lee fighting off an attacking EAGLE with kungfu

F - Effluent- Joyce - environmentalists joyfully finding a plant by an EFFLUENT pipe

G - Jeans - Nietzche - a holey pair of JEANS with a knee showing through

H - H-Bomb - Kafka - a grey civil service CAFe being blown up by an H-Bomb etc.

Key Points

The Alphabet Technique links the items to be remembered with images of the letters A-Z. This allows you to remember a medium length list in the correct order. By pegging the items to be remembered to letters of the alphabet you know if you have forgotten items, and know the cues to use to trigger their recall.

The Journey System: Remembering Long Lists

The journey method is a powerful, flexible and effective mnemonic based around the idea of remembering landmarks on a well-known journey. It combines the narrative flow of the Link Method and the structure and order of the Peg Systems into one very powerful system.

How to Use the Tool:

You use the Journey Method by associating information with landmarks on a journey that you know well. This could, for example, be your journey to work in the morning; the route you use to get to the front door when you get up; the route to visit your parents; or a tour around a holiday destination.

Once you are familiar with the technique you may be able to create imaginary journeys that fix in your mind, and apply these.

To use this technique most effectively, it is often best to prepare the journey beforehand. In this way the landmarks are clear in your mind before you try to commit information to them.

One of the ways of doing this is to write down all the landmarks that you can recall in order on a piece of paper. This allows you to fix these landmarks as the significant ones to be used in your mnemonic, separating them from others that you may notice as you get to know the route even better.

To remember a list of items, whether these are people, experiments, events or objects, all you need do is associate these things with the landmarks or stops on your journey.

This is an extremely effective method of remembering long lists of information.

With a sufficiently long journey you could, for example, remember elements on the periodic table, lists of Kings and Presidents, geographical information, or the order of cards in a shuffled pack.

The system is extremely flexible: all you need do to remember many items is to remember a longer journey with more landmarks. To remember a short list, only use part of the route!

One advantage of this technique is that you can use it to work both backwards and forwards, and start anywhere within the route to retrieve information.

You can use the technique well with other mnemonics. This can be done either by building complex coding images at the stops on a journey, or by linking to other mnemonics at each stop.

You could start other journeys at each landmark. Alternatively, you may use a peg system to organise lists of journeys, etc.

Example:

You may, as a simple example, want to remember something mundane like this shopping list:

Coffee, salad, vegetables, bread, kitchen paper, fish, chicken breasts, pork chops, soup, fruit, bath tub cleaner.

You could associate this list with a journey to a supermarket. Mnemonic images could be:

1. *Front door:* spilt coffee grains on the doormat

2. *Rose bush in front garden:* growing lettuce leaves and tomatoes around the roses
3. *Car:* with potatoes, onions and cauliflower on the driver's seat
4. *End of the road:* an arch of French bread over the road
5. *Past garage:* with its sign wrapped in kitchen roll
6. *Under railway bridge:* from which haddock and cod are dangling by their tails
7. *Traffic lights*: chickens squawking and flapping on top of lights
8. *Past church:* in front of which a pig is doing karate, breaking boards
9. *Under office block:* with a soup slick underneath: my car tires send up jets of tomato soup as I drive through it
10. *Past car park:* with apples and oranges tumbling from the top level
11. *Supermarket car park:* a filthy bath tub is parked in the space next to my car!

Key Points

The journey method is a powerful, effective method of remembering lists of information, by imagining images and events at stops on a journey.

As the journeys used are distinct in location and form, one list remembered using this technique is easy to distinguish from other lists.

To use this technique you need to invest some time in preparing journeys clearly in your mind. This investment pays off many times over by the application of the technique.

The Roman Room System: Remembering Grouped Information

The Roman Room technique, also known as the Method of Loci, is an ancient and effective way of remembering information where its structure is not important. As an example, it serves as the basis of one of the powerful mnemonic systems used to learn languages.

How to Use the Tool:

To use the technique, imagine a room that you know, such as your sitting room, bedroom, office or classroom. Within the room are objects. Associate images representing the information you want to remember with the objects in the room. To recall information, simply take a tour around the room in your mind, visualising the known objects and their associated images.

The technique can be expanded by going into more detail, and keying information to be remembered to smaller objects. Alternatively you can open doors from your room into other rooms and use the objects in them as well.

As you need them, you can build extensions to your rooms in your imagination, and fill them with objects that would logically be there.

You can use other rooms to store other categories of information.

There is no need to restrict this information to rooms: you could use a landscape or a town you know well, and populate it with memory images.

The Roman Room technique is just one way of

representing your cognitive map of the information in an easily accessible way.

Example:

For example, I can use my sitting room as a basis for the technique. In this room I have the following objects:

Table, lamp, sofa, large bookcase, small bookcase, CD rack, telephone, television, DVD player, chair, mirror, black and white photographs, etc.

I may want to remember a list of World War I war poets:

Rupert Brooke, G.K. Chesterton, Walter de la Mare, Robert Graves, Rudyard Kipling, Wilfred Owen, Siegfried Sassoon, W.B. Yates.

I could visualise walking through my front door. Within this image, someone has painted a picture on it showing a scene from the Battle of the Somme. In the centre of the picture is a man sitting in a trench writing in a dirty exercise book.

I walk into the sitting room, and look at the table. On the top is RUPERT the Bear sitting in a small BROOK (we do not need to worry about where the water goes in our imagination!) These codes for Rupert Brooke.

Someone seems to have done some moving: a CHEST has been left on the sofa. Some jeans (Alphabet System: G=Jeans) are hanging out of one drawer, and some cake has been left on the top (K=Cake). This code for G K Chesterton.

The lamp has a small statuette of a brick WALL over which a female horse (MARE) is jumping. These codes for Walter de la Mare.

Key Points

The Roman Room technique is similar to the Journey method. It works by pegging images coding for information to known things, in this case to objects in a room.

The Roman Room technique is most effective for storing lists of unlinked information, while the journey method is better for storing lists of ordered items.

The Major System: Remembering Very Long Numbers

The Major Memory System is one of the most powerful memory systems available. It takes a lot of time to master, but once learned is very powerful. The technique often forms the basis of some of the extraordinary, almost magical, memory feats performed by stage magicians and memory performers.

The system works by converting number sequences into nouns, nouns into images, and linking images into sequences. These sequences can be very complex and detailed.

How to Use the Tool:

The building blocks of the system are the association of the numbers below with the following consonant sounds:

0 - s, z, soft-c - remember as 'z is first letter of zero'

1 - d, t, th - remember as letters with 1 downstroke

2 - n - remember as having 2 downstrokes

3 - m - has three downstrokes

4 - r - imagine a 4 and an R glued together back-to-back

5 - L - imagine the 5 propped up against a book end (L)

6 - j, sh, soft-ch, dg, soft-g - g is 6 rotated 180 degrees.

7 - k, hard-ch, hard-c, hard-g, ng - imagine K as two 7s rotated and glued together

8 - f, v - imagine the bottom loop of the 8 as an eFfluent pipe discharging waste (letter image of F in alphabet system)

9 - p, b - b as 9 rotated 180 degrees.

These associations need to be learned thoroughly before going further with the technique.

Starting to use the Major System

The system operates on a number of levels, depending on the amount of time you are prepared to devote to learning the system.

The first level, which involves coding single digit numbers into small words, functions almost as a poor relation of the number/rhyme system. It is at higher levels that you can unleash the real power of the system. You should, however, learn to use this first level before moving on.

The trick with converting numbers into words is to use only the consonants that code information within the word, while using vowels to pad the consonants out with meaning. If you do have to use other consonants to make up a word, use only those that do not code for numbers - i.e. h, q, w, x, and y.

At the first level we code each number into a short noun.

This is made up of the consonant coding for the number, and vowels that turn the consonant into a word.

On a sheet of paper, write the numbers 0 to 9, and apply these rules to create your own memory words. Some examples are shown below:

0 - saw

1 - toe

2 - neigh

3 - ma

4 - ray

5 - law

6 - jaw

7 - key

8 - fee

9 - pie

You can use these words in association much like the other peg technique memory words.

Moving to the Second Level

Similar rules apply to creating a standard word from two numbers. It is best not to try to use a single number word as a root, as this can confuse the image.

Write down the numbers 01 to 99, and apply the rules to create memory words for yourself.

A few examples are shown below:

09 - z, p - zap

17 - t, ch - tech

23 - n, m - name

36 - m, sh - mesh

41 - r,s - rose

52 - l, n - line

64 - ch, r - chair

75 - k, l - keel

89 - f, p - fop

98 - b, f - beef

Taking the Major System Further

Just using double number words may be enough to make this a sufficiently powerful mnemonic for you. Alternatively you may decide to use triple number words, using the same construction rules as double number words.

Examples:

182 - d, v, n - Devon

304 - m, s, r - miser

400 - r, c, s - races

651 - j, l, d - jellied

801 - f, z, d - fazed

Even though you can construct words from first principles each time, at this level of complexity it may be worth writing them down to make them easier to remember.

You can then run through them many times to strengthen the link in your mind between the numbers and the associated words. This will help you to remember the appropriate word faster.

Using Words to Remember Long Numbers

Once you have come up with words and images to link to your numbers, you can start to apply the technique to remember, for example, long numbers. A good way of doing this is to associate Major System words with stops on a journey.

Example:

The number Pi is 3.14159265359 (to 11 decimal places). Using the major system and the journey system together, I can remember this as:

- Passing my Ma (3) by the front door of my house
- Seeing that someone has dared (1,4,1) to sleep under the rose bush in the garden
- Someone has tied a loop (5,9) of yellow ribbon onto the steering wheel of my car
- I see a poster with a photo of a steaming pile of sausages and mashed potato, with the title 'glorious NOSH' (2,6) at the end of the road
- A lama (5,3) is grazing on grass outside the garage forecourt
- Another loop (5,9) of yellow ribbon has been tied around the railway bridge. This is getting strange!

Key Points

The major memory system works by linking numbers to consonants, and then by linking these into words. By using the images these words create, and linking them together with the journey system, large amounts of information can be accurately memorised.

Using Concept Maps or Mind Maps to Remember Structured Information

How to Use the Tool:

Mind Maps are not formally mnemonics. They do, however, help you to lay out the structure of a topic as a clear 'shape' that you can remember easily. By seeing this shape in your mind, you can prompt yourself to remember the information coded within it. This becomes even easier if you have coded this information using striking images.

Memory Games: Have fun, while you improve your memory!

Have you ever looked up a phone number and repeated it over and over to yourself until you dialled it correctly? This draws on your working memory; however, just moments after dialling the telephone number, chances are you have forgotten it.

This is because the telephone number was not "committed" to your long-term memory. And, while working memory is reliable for quick recall of bits of information (like phone numbers), it can hold only a few pieces of information and only for a very short time.

To remember things for a longer amount of time, you must connect the new information with information you already have, "committing" it to your long-term memory, which stores more information and, for a longer period of time.

There are, of course, many 'serious' techniques for improving your memory.

Story Telling

One way to remember the information you need to commit to long-term memory is to make up a story that "connects" the items or facts you need to remember, thus making them easier to recall. The idea here is that it's easier to remember more information when one fact or item connects to another.

While making up the story, create a strong mental image of what's happening. This helps to "connect" the data to an image and better cement it in your long-term memory.

It's fun to practice using this technique in a group. Practice by laying out 20 or more objects on the table and trying to remember them. Each member of the group takes his or her turn to add to the story by including another object.

If the first three objects are an apple, a key and a mobile phone, here's how the story might start:

Person 1: In the orchard, ripe apples were falling from the trees.

Person 2: But the gate to the orchard was locked and John had brought the wrong key.

Person 3: So he called Sue from his mobile phone to see if she could help.....

Once all the objects have been included in the story, remove them all from the room. See who can remember the most items.

Now tell the story again as a group, taking it in turns. The group will probably be able to remember the whole story and so recall all the items.

Pexeso: Matching Pairs

Pexeso involves matching pairs of like cards or tiles from a large group, when one of each group is hidden.

You play Pexeso with a set of cards or tiles that includes pairs of picture or numbers. You can play using half a pack of standard playing cards – just remove 2 of the 4 suits, so you have just 2 aces, 2 kings, 2 queens and so on.

Start by laying out 24 of the cards, making sure the 24 cards consists of 12 matched pairs. Once face down, move the cards around so that you do not know where any single card is located.

Turn one card over at a time, take a look at the number or object, and then turn it face down again. Repeat this process until you turn over a card that matches a card you turned over earlier. Now find the card's 'mate' by remembering from earlier where it is located. As you find a matched pair, remove them from the group. The number of cards dwindles until all the pairs are matched.

Time yourself and see how you improve (get faster) each time you play.

As you get better, increase the number of cards you start with, moving from the original 24 to 30, then to 36, 42 and so on.

'Blind' Jigsaw Puzzles

Another fun and inexpensive way to give your concentration and memory a boost is the good old-fashioned jigsaw puzzle.

Playing it 'blind' means without referring back to the picture on the box!

First, look at a picture of the completed puzzle. Give yourself a few minutes to commit it to memory.

Next, mix up the pieces to the jigsaw puzzle.

Now, work to put it back together without looking at the picture of the completed puzzle again (until you are done).

Trivia Quizzes

A great way to improve how well you recall information is to play trivia quizzes. The trivia can be about anything – movies, history, even about your specific business.

Whilst you can easily purchase trivia quiz board games and books, you can also make up your own questions when you are playing in a group.

Each person submits a list of questions (and answers!) and then to 'quiz master' takes questions from each person's list in turn.

When you play with a new set of trivia questions, you rely on your recall of prior knowledge and experience to find the answers. If you play with the same questions in a few days or weeks later, you will also rely on memory of playing the game last time. Both new questions and re-runs are good for building you memory skills.

How to Learn a Foreign Language

Using the Tools:

Foreign languages are the ideal subject area for the use of memory techniques. Learning vocabulary is often a matter of associating a meaningless collection of syllables with a word in your own language.

Traditionally people have associated these words by repetition – by saying the word in their own language and the foreign language time and time and time and time again. You can improve on this tedious way of learning by using three good techniques:

1. Using Mnemonics to Link Words

This is a simple extension of the link method. Here you are using images to link a word in your own language with a word in a foreign language.

For example, in learning English/French vocabulary:

- English: rug/carpet - French: tapis - imagine an ornate oriental carpet with a tap as the central design woven in chrome thread
- English: grumpy - French: grognon - a grumpy man groaning with irritation
- English: to tease - French: taquiner - a woman teasing her husband as she takes in the washing.

This technique was formalised by Dr. Michael Gruneberg, and is known as the 'LinkWord' technique. He has produced language books (an example is German by Association) in many language pairs to help students acquire the basic vocabulary needed to get by in the language (usually about 1000 words). It is claimed that using this technique this basic vocabulary can be learned in just 10 hours.

2. The Town Language Mnemonic

This is a very elegant, effective mnemonic that fuses a

sophisticated variant of the Roman Room system with the system described above.

This depends on the fact that the basic vocabulary of a language relates to everyday things: things that you can usually find in a city, town or village. To use the technique, choose a town that you are very familiar with. Use objects within that place as the cues to recall the images that link to foreign words.

Nouns in the town:

Nouns should be associated to the most relevant locations: for example, the image coding the foreign word for book could be associated with a book on a shelf in the library. You could associate the word for bread with an image of a loaf in a baker's shop.

Words for vegetables could be associated with parts of a display outside a greengrocer's. Perhaps there is a farm just outside the town that allows all the animal name associations to be made.

Adjectives in the park:

Adjectives can be associated with a garden or park within the town: words such as green, smelly, bright, small, cold, etc. can be easily related to objects in a park.

Perhaps there is a pond there, or a small wood, or perhaps people with different characteristics are walking around.

Verbs in the sports centre:

Verbs can most easily be associated with a sports centre or playing field.

This allows us all the associations of lifting, running, walking, hitting, eating, swimming, driving, etc.

Remembering Genders

In a language where gender is important, a very good method of remembering this is to divide your town into two main zones. In one zone you code information on masculine gender nouns, while in the other zone you code information on feminine nouns.

Where the language has a neutral gender, then use three zones. You can separate these areas with busy roads, rivers, etc. To fix the gender of a noun, simply associate its image with a place in the correct part of town. This makes remembering genders easy!

Many Languages, many towns

Another elegant spin-off of the technique comes when learning several languages: normally this can cause confusion. With the town mnemonic, all you need do is choose a different city, town or village for each language to be learned. Ideally this might be in the relevant country. Practically, however, you might just decide to use a local town with the appropriate foreign flavour.

3. The 100 Most Common Words

Tony Buzan, in his book 'Using your Memory', points out that just 100 words comprise 50% of all words used in conversation in a language. Learning these core 100 words gets you a long way towards being able to speak in that language, albeit at a basic level. The 100 basic words used in conversation are shown below:

1. A/an	2. After	3. Again

4. All	5. Almost	6. Also
7. Always	8. And	9. Because
10. Before	11. Big	12. But
13. (I) can	14. (I) come	15. Either/or
16. (I) find	17. First	18. For
19. Friend	20. From	21. (I) go
22. Good	23. Good-bye	24. Happy
25. (I) have	26. He	27. Hello
28. Here	29. How	30. I
31. (I) am	32. If	33. In
34. (I) know	35. Last	36. (I) like
37. Little	38. (I) love	39. (I) make
40. Many	41. One	42. More
43. Most	44. Much	45. My
46. New	47. No	48. Not
49. Now	50. Of	51. Often
52. On	53. One	54. Only
55. Or	56. Other	57. Our
58. Out	59. Over	60. People
61. Place	62. Please	63. Same
64. (I) see	65. She	66. So
67. Some	68. Sometimes	69. Still

70. Such	71. (I) tell	72. Thank you
73. That	74. The	75. Their
76. Them	77. Then	78. There is
79. They	80. Thing	81. (I) think
82. This	83. Time	84. To
85. Under	86. Up	87. Us
88. (I) use	89. Very	90. We
91. What	92. When	93. Where
94. Which	95. Who	96. Why
97. With	98. Yes	99. You
100. Your		

Summary

The three approaches to learning foreign languages shown here can be very effective. They help to:

- Point out the most important words to learn
- Show how to link words in your own language to words in a foreign language, and
- Show how to structure recall of the language through use of the town mnemonic.

How to Remember Information for Exams

Using the Tools:

A very effective way of structuring information for revision is to draw up a full, colour-coded concept or memory map of a subject. This will help you to see the overall structure of the topic and show you the associations between pieces of information. A good concept map can be an effective mnemonic in its own right.

The problem with this is that you can forget the label on a line on a concept map. A more reliable method is to take your concept map, and break it down into a numbered list of important points. You can then use one of the peg techniques to remember the items on the list. Alternatively you can use the journey technique for longer lists.

By associating items on a list with a peg system or journey, you can check that you have retrieved all items held by the mnemonic.

Supporting facts can be associated into images or sub-mnemonics. These could be triggered by the pegs for the peg systems, or at landmarks if you use the journey system. Alternatively you can loosely associate this information with the facts coded.

Retrieving all the facts necessary to answer an exam essay question becomes as simple as running through the mnemonic in your mind. As you go, jot down the retrieved facts that are relevant to the question.

Once you have written these down, you can apply any other mnemonics you have coded, or note any associated facts and connections that occur to you. This should ensure that you have all possible information available to you, and should help you to produce a good essay plan.

How to Remember People's Names

Using the Tools:

Remembering people's names needs a slightly different approach from all the others explained so far in this section. The techniques used, though, are quite simple:

1. Face Association

Examine a person's face discretely when you are introduced. Try to find an unusual feature, whether ears, hairline, forehead, eyebrows, eyes, nose, mouth, chin, complexion, etc.

Create an association between that characteristic, the face, and the name in your mind. The association may be to link the person with someone else you know with the same name.

Alternatively it may be to associate a rhyme or image of the name with the person's face or defining feature.

2. Repetition

When you are introduced, ask for the person to repeat their name. Use the name yourself as often as possible (without overdoing it!).

If it is unusual, ask how it is spelled or where it is comes from, and if appropriate, exchange cards. Keep in mind that the more often you hear and see the name, the more likely it is to sink in.

Also, after you have left that person's company, review the name in your mind several times. If you are particularly keen you might decide to write it down and make notes.

Summary

The methods suggested for remembering names are fairly simple and obvious, but are useful. Association either with images of a name or with other people can really help. Repetition and review help to confirm your memory.

An important thing to stress is practice, patience, and progressive improvement.

How to Remember Lists and Long Numbers

Using the Tools:

Remembering lists are what many mnemonics are for. You can code almost any information into these mnemonic lists. All that you need is the imagination to come up with the relevant associations.

To memorise short lists, use:

- The Link or Story Methods
- The Number/Rhyme System, or
- The Number/Shape Method

To remember intermediate and longer lists, use:

- The Alphabet Technique, or
- The Journey Technique

As with lists, using mnemonic systems, remembering numbers becomes extremely simple. There are a number of approaches, depending on the types of numbers being remembered:

1. Short numbers

The easiest, but least reliable, way of remembering numbers

is to use simple Number/Rhyme images associated in a story.

A better way is to use a simple peg system, where, for example, you can associate digits from the Number/Rhyme System into positions organised with the Alphabet System.

2. Long numbers (e.g. Pi)

You can store long numbers most effectively with the Journey System. At a simple level, single numbers can be stored at each stop on the journey using Number/Rhyme or Number/Shape images. At a more advanced level you can increase the number of digits stored at each stop by using the Major System.

By using all the simple techniques together you should be able to store a 100 digit number with relatively little effort. Using the more powerful systems, holding it to 1000 digits might not be too much of a challenge.

3. Telephone Numbers

These can be remembered simply by associating numbers from the Number/Rhyme system with positions in either the Alphabet Technique or the Journey System. You can then associate these with the face or name of the person whose number you are remembering.

For example, to remember that someone's phone number is 735-3458, I can imagine myself traveling to their flat: with my destination firmly in mind, I envisage the following stops on my journey:

1. Front door: the door has sprouted angel's wings, and is flying up to heaven! (7)

2. Rose bush: a small sapling (tree, 3) is growing its way through the middle of the bush.
3. Car: some bees have started to build a hive (5) under the wheel of my car. I have to move it very carefully to avoid damaging it.
4. End of road: a tree (3) has fallen into the road. I have to drive around it.
5. Past garage: Someone has nailed a door (4) to the sign. Strange!
6. Under railway bridge: the bees are building another hive (5) between the girders!
7. Beside the river: A rusty farm gate (8) is blocking the road.

■■■

CHAPTER 7

Easy Tips for Improving Memory

Do you feel that you have a poor memory? You may just have some less-than-effective habits when it comes to taking in and processing information. Barring disease, disorder, or injury, you can improve your ability to learn and retain information.

It's a classic situation – you meet someone new, and then moments later you've forgotten their name! Names, passwords, pin and telephone numbers... the list is endless – with so much to memorize is it really possible to improve how much you can remember?

The good news is "yes"! Just like every muscle in your body, the adage "use it or lose it" applies, so the more you exercise your brain, the more you will remember.

The well known learning curve shows that in five minutes, much of the information we have taken in is lost. After an hour - two thirds of it is lost. And after a day has passed - 90 % of it is lost.

This is the curve of forgetting. What we've found is that

you can reverse that curve. And there are various techniques to do it.

The first thing we want to go over is how a simple recall method can help you store the information. Now this is information that we'll call ROTE INFORMATION for example, when you are learning a section of a speech. In these cases you are learning something that is not just a list, that is not just something simple and direct. Its more of a instance of wanting to remember situations – wanting to remember broader terms.

For this, we are going to use a little bit of ASSOCIATION but then we are going to base it primarily on MEMORY REVIEW. This works whether you are remembering lines of poetry or outlines of the sensory system.

First and foremost you want to ORGANIZE the information you are going to be taking in. You have to decide in what manner you want to take the information in. It may be by rote memorization of a section. It may well be some type of outline form.

The first step is to take in the information. And when you take in the information you really must learn to fully attend to what you are doing. Involve yourself in what your taking in. WE use the phrase "Be where you are." Be truly focused.Incorporate as many of the senses as you can. In other words, write it down, see it, even say it out loud sometimes. The more senses involved enhance the memory process.

And now you can reverse the learning curve. This is the key point here. You can reverse the learning curve by RECALL. The number of times you recall something helps move that piece of information from your short-term memory to your long-term memory.

To point out a specific technique that works the best:

Step number 1 - take in formation.

Step number 2 - about five minutes later, undisturbed, go over the main points of what you are trying to remember. That should only take you a minute or two.

Step number 3 - an hour later, do the same thing.

Step number 4 - three hours later, do the same thing. Just go back over the information a minute or two.

Step number 5 - six hours later, do the same thing. Then that night before you go to sleep, review the material one last time.

Then step number 6 - repeat that three times a day for the second and third days. Now you have that information for the long-term.

Now to the student first taking this in sitting there saying, Man, I'm not going to do that. That six times the first day, two to three times the next day. My goodness, there's no way I'm going to do that. That's just a lot of work.

Baloney! Think about it. That's 12 times the first day. The second and third days, you only do it 6 times. That's eighteen, let's round it to twenty times. That's twenty times you are reviewing that information over three days for a minute or two. That means you are spending forty minutes studying that information, and you have it. And you know it, you possess it, and it isn't going anywhere. How many hours do people spend studying? Think about it. Typically, people sit down and study a subject for an hour or more to try to learn it. This is simply a more efficient way of doing it in a more piecemeal fashion. And by spreading it out over a period of days and recalling it more and more, you move it into that long-term memory and it stays solidly there.

OK, that's where we are talking about memorizing, rote memorizing, where we are trying to take in broader or larger pieces of information.

Top Ten List

Lets say we are trying to remember items. We are working with lists. Now there are a number of ways to do this. The two ways we've found we really like best. We'll call the first one the TOP TEN LIST. With the top ten list, you are taking something familiar, something that you know about, and something that isn't going anywhere, and you use that as a frame work for pegging items. We are going to be working with associations. You are going to be associating something with these pegs. Whether it is an item or whether it is a feeling, whether it is a person, it's going to be a form of ASSOCIATON. And remember that more we involve the senses, the more we can see, feel, smell, taste, these memories, the better we are going to remember. We also want to incorporate a little bit of exaggeration in here. Because the more bizarre, the more silly things are, the more outlandish things are, the more we take note of it, the easier we will remember it.

For the top ten list, let's use our bodies. Because it isn't going anywhere and we are very familiar with it. Let's start at the bottom and work our way up.

Number ONE - we are going to use our TOES.

Then we are going to use our KNEE for number TWO.

Number THREE - we are going to use the THIGH MUSCLE, right above the knee, that quadriceps up there.

OK now ONE was the TOES, TWO is the KNEE, THREE is the THIGH MUSCLE. So you are just working your way up.

Number FOUR, we are going to call that our REAR END. That is our seat, our rear end. Everybody has one.

Number FIVE is going to be the LOVE HANDLES, that little bulge of extra flesh that you have along the sides of your abdomen.

Number SIX will be your SHOULDERS.

Number SEVEN - your COLLAR. The collar of your shirt around your neck.

Number EIGHT is going to be your FACE.

Number NINE is going to be the TOP OF YOUR HEAD - the point of your head.

Number TEN, that is going to be the CEILING up above your head.

OK lets say we want to remember the following list: toaster, butterfly, ejection, wink, Mediterranean, Volvo, wolf, slither, tree, and incision. A pretty bizarre set of words. Lets see how we are going to remember these words using our top ten list.

Well, first thing we are going to do - we are going to remember that toaster. We are going to put that TOASTER on our TOES. We are going to think about that toaster bouncing on our toes. We are going to flip it up in the air with our toes.

Then we have a butterfly - this is going to be an easy one. The BUTTERFLY lands on your KNEE. You can see it crawling around on your knee.

This next one is EJECTION, with the thigh. Well lets see, how are we going to remember this? The way we're going to remember it is if someone wants to be ejected from a plane, They're going to be pushing out with their legs. We're going to be pushing with our legs. Our THIGH MUSCLES are going to be flexing to eject us from that plane.

OK now, wink. This one is going to be pretty easy. Somebody has got a cute REAR END, so we are going to WINK.

The Mediterranean - how are we going to associate the Mediterranean with love handles? Well let's think about it. We are going lolling out by the Mediterranean, sunning by the MEDITERRANEAN, we don't want to have LOVE HANDLES hanging way out over the edge of our belt.

Volvo - how are we going to do Volvo with shoulders? Well, let's say we are going to carry that VOLVO on our SHOULDERS.

And a wolf? A WOLF may want to bite you around the COLLAR, bite you around the neck. You have got to be careful. You don't want that wolf to bite you there.

And a sliver - let's say you have got a SLIVER of wood that's stuck in the side of your FACE a little bit - and you have got to pull it out with tweezers.

Then a tree. OK, that's pretty easy. We've got a TREE growing out of the TOP OF OUR HEAD.

And an incision - we're going to make an INCISION in that CEILING, and where we make an incision in that ceiling, all the insulation is going to come out on us.

OK, now we have got our facts. Sit down and think about it. Remember that toaster on your toes. Remember that butterfly on your knee. See you can do this without even going back to the list. You are going to eject from the seat by using your thighs.

Someone is going to wink at someone who has a cute rear end. You don't want those love handles on the Mediterranean. That Volvo is really weighing down your shoulders. That sliver that is in your cheek - you've got to be careful taking it out with the tweezers. You have got a tree growing out of the top of your head. And now, guess what we've got? We've got an incision in the ceiling letting everything fall down on us.

That's how easy it is to use the top ten list. You can use this when you need to remember lists of things or when you have things you want to do. You have that top ten list, that set of little pegs walking around with you all the time now. The way you are going to get better at using the top ten list is to practice it. Yes, use it for school, but you can also get used to using it for lists of things you may want to get at the store, lists of things you have to do that day, even lists of people you have got to write notes to. Whatever the list might be, get used to using it because as you practice it, you get better and better at it.

Other Memory Improving Tips

Practice the memory techniques below and improve your recall of information, increase the speed with which you can learn, remember detailed, structured information and, yes, new names too!

1. **Convince yourself that you do have a good memory that will improve:** Too many people get stuck here and convince themselves that their memory is bad, that they are just not good with names, that numbers just slip out of their minds for some reason. Erase those thoughts and vow to improve your memory. Commit yourself to the task and bask in your achievements — it's hard to keep motivated if you beat yourself down every time you make a little bit of progress.
2. **Exercise your brain:** Regularly "exercising" the brain keeps it growing and spurs the development of new nerve connections that can help improve memory. By developing new mental skills—especially complex ones such as learning a new language or learning to play a new musical instrument—and challenging your brain with puzzles and games you can keep your brain active and improve its physiological functioning. Try some puzzle exercises everyday such as word cross, sudoku and some other games as easy to put into your mobile phone and practise it maybe once for 30 minutes per day.
3. **Exercise daily:** Regular aerobic exercise improves circulation and efficiency throughout the body, including in the brain, and can help ward off the memory loss that comes with aging. Exercise also makes you more alert and relaxed, and can thereby improve your memory uptake, allowing you to take better mental "pictures."
4. **Reduce stress:** Chronic stress, although it does not physically damage the brain, can make remembering much

more difficult. After prolonged stress the brain will be damaged. Stressful situations are recognized by the hypothalamus, which in turn signals the pituitary gland. The pituitary gland secreted adrenocorticotropic hormone (ACTH)which influences the adrenal glands to secrete adrenaline and later cortisol(corticosteroids). The corticosteroids can weaken the blood-brain barrier and damage the hippocampus(the memory center). Ironically, the hippocampus controls the secretion of the hormone released by the hypothalamus through a process of negative feedback. After chronic stress it will be damaged and it will not be as efficient in regulating the degenerative corticosteroids and memory will be harmed. Neurogenesis (formation of new neurons) indeed exists in the hippocampus but stress inhibits it. To recapitulate and synthesis, chronic stress will affect your health and your memory, it will damage the brain so the best option is to learn to control stress. Stress will never be eliminated, but it definitely can be controlled. Even temporary stresses can make it more difficult to effectively focus on concepts and observe things. Try to relax, regularly practice yoga or other stretching exercises, and see a doctor if you have severe chronic stress as soon as possible.

5. **Eat well and eat right:** There are a lot of herbal supplements on the market that claim to improve memory, but none have yet been shown to be effective in clinical tests (although small studies have shown some promising results for ginkgo biloba and phosphatidylserine). A healthy diet, however, contributes to a healthy brain, and foods containing antioxidants—broccoli, blueberries, spinach, and berries, for example—and Omega-3 fatty acids

appear to promote healthy brain functioning. Feed your brain with such supplements as Thiamine, Vitamin E, Niacin and Vitamin B-6. Grazing, eating 5 or 6 small meals throughout the day instead of 3 large meals, also seems to improve mental functioning (including memory) by limiting dips in blood sugar, which may negatively affect the brain.

6. **Take better pictures:** Often we forget things not because our memory is bad, but rather because our observational skills need work. One common situation where this occurs (and which almost everyone can relate to) is meeting new people. Often we don't really learn people's names at first because we aren't really concentrating on remembering them. You'll find that if you make a conscious effort to remember such things, you'll do much better. One way to train yourself to be more observant is to look at an unfamiliar photograph for a few seconds and then turn the photograph over and describe or write down as many details as you can about the photograph. Try closing your eyes and picturing the photo in your mind. Use a new photograph each time you try this exercise, and with regular practice you will find you're able to remember more details with even shorter glimpses of the photos.

7. **Give yourself time to form a memory:** Memories are very fragile in the short-term, and distractions can make you quickly forget something as simple as a phone number. The key to avoid losing memories before you can even form them is to be able to focus on the thing to be remembered for a while without thinking about other things, so when you're trying to remember something, avoid distractions and complicated tasks for a few minutes.

8. **Create vivid, memorable images:** You remember information more easily if you can visualise it. If you want to associate a child with a book, try not to visualise the child reading the book – that's too simple and forgettable. Instead, come up with something more jarring, something that sticks, like the book chasing the child, or the child eating the book. It's your mind – make the images as shocking and emotional as possible to keep the associations strong.
9. **Repeat things you need to learn:** The more times you hear, see, or think about something, the more surely you'll remember it, right? It's a no-brainer. When you want to remember something, be it your new coworker's name or your best friend's birthday, repeat it, either out loud or silently. Try writing it down; think about it.
10. **Group things you need to remember:** Random lists of things (a shopping list, for example) can be especially difficult to remember. To make it easier, try categorizing the individual things from the list. If you can remember that, among other things, you wanted to buy four different kinds of vegetables, you'll find it easier to remember all four.
11. **Organise your life:** Keep items that you frequently need, such as keys and eyeglasses, in the same place every time. Use an electronic organizer or daily planner to keep track of appointments, due dates for bills, and other tasks. Keep phone numbers and addresses in an address book or enter them into your computer or cell phone. Improved organisation can help free up your powers of concentration so that you can remember less routine things. Even if being organized doesn't improve your memory, you'll receive a

lot of the same benefits (i.e. you won't have to search for your keys anymore).

12. **Try meditation:** Research now suggests that people who regularly practice "mindfulness" meditation are able to focus better and may have better memories. Mindfulness (also known as awareness or insight meditation) is the type commonly practiced in Western countries and is easy to learn. Studies at Massachusetts General Hospital show that regular meditation thickens the cerebral cortex in the brain by increasing the blood flow to that region. Some researchers believe this can enhance attention span, focus, and memory.
13. **Sleep well:** The amount of sleep we get affects the brain's ability to recall recently learned information. Getting a good night's sleep – a minimum of seven hours a night – may improve your short-term memory and long-term relational memory, according to recent studies conducted at the Harvard Medical School.
14. **Build your memorization arsenal:** Learn pegs, memory palaces, and the Dominic System. These techniques form the foundation for mnemonic techniques, and will visibly improve your memory.
15. **Venture out and learn from your mistakes:** Go ahead and take a stab at memorizing the first one hundred digits of pi, or, if you've done that already, the first one thousand. Memorize the monarchs of England through your memory palaces, or your grocery list through visualization. Through diligent effort you will eventually master the art of memorisation.

■■■

More titles are available in

General Books Series

1. A Handbook of Etiquettes **(New)**
2. How to Beat Your Competitors **(New)**
3. The World's Great Scientists **(New)**
4. The Kama Sutra of Mallinga Vatsyayana **(New)**
5. How to Negotiate Effectively **(New)**
6. Vatsyayana's Kamasutra Select **(New)**
7. Patriot: The Unique Indian Leader
   Netaji Subhas Chander Bose
8. Body Language **(New)**
9. Art of Successful Living **(New)**
10. Make Your Boss Happy **(New)**
11. Jokes for All **(New)**
12. Selected Dohas **(New)**
13. Baby Names for Girls **(New)**
14. Baby Names for Boys **(New)**
15. Art of Public Speaking **(New)**
16. The World's Greatest Speeches **(New)**
17. Group Discussions **(New)**
18. Personality Development **(New)**
19. Think Positive & Things Will Go Right **(New)**
20. Once in a Blue Moon (A Tantra Tale) **(New)**

21. God is Dead **(New)**

22. Travel India
(A Complete Guide to Tourists) **(New)**

23. Glimpses of Urdu Poetry **(New)**

24. Indian Mythology (PB) **(New)**

25. Helpline for Stressed Parents

26. Grow Rich with Peace of Mind

27. How to be Fit & Young

28. How to Succeed in Life

29. How to Reduce Tension

30. A Book of Stenography

31. Business Letters

32. Baby Names for Boys

33. Baby Names for Girls

34. Indian National Congress

Lotus PRESS